EURIPIDES III

HERACLES

THE TROJAN WOMEN

IPHIGENIA AMONG THE TAURIANS

ION

THE COMPLETE GREEK TRAGEDIES
Edited by David Grene & Richmond Lattimore
THIRD EDITION *Edited by Mark Griffith & Glenn W. Most*

EURIPIDES III

HERACLES *Translated by William Arrowsmith*

THE TROJAN WOMEN *Translated by Richmond Lattimore*

IPHIGENIA AMONG THE TAURIANS *Translated by Anne Carson*

ION *Translated by Ronald Frederick Willetts*

The University of Chicago Press CHICAGO & LONDON

MARK GRIFFITH is professor of classics and of theater, dance, and performance studies at the University of California, Berkeley.

GLENN W. MOST is professor of ancient Greek at the Scuola Normale Superiore at Pisa and a visiting member of the Committee on Social Thought at the University of Chicago.

DAVID GRENE (1913–2002) taught classics for many years at the University of Chicago.

RICHMOND LATTIMORE (1906–1984), professor of Greek at Bryn Mawr College, was a poet and translator best known for his translations of the Greek classics, especially his versions of the *Iliad* and *Odyssey*.

The University of Chicago Press, Chicago 60637
The University of Chicago Press, Ltd., London
© 2013 by The University of Chicago

Heracles © 1956, 2013 by the University of Chicago
The Trojan Women © 1947 by the Dial Press; © 1958, 2013 by the University of Chicago
Ion © 1958, 2013 by the University of Chicago
Iphigenia among the Taurians © 2013 by Anne Carson

Printed and bound by CPI Group (UK) Ltd, Croydon, CR0 4YY

22 21 20 19 18 17 16 15   3 4 5

ISBN-13: 978-0-226-30881-4 (cloth)
ISBN-13: 978-0-226-30882-1 (paper)
ISBN-13: 978-0-226-30936-1 (e-book)
ISBN-10: 0-226-30881-2 (cloth)
ISBN-10: 0-226-30882-0 (paper)
ISBN-10: 0-226-30936-3 (e-book)

Library of Congress Cataloging-in-Publication Data
Euripides.
  [Works. English. 2012]
  Euripedes — Third edition.
  volumes cm. — (the complete Greek tragedies)
  ISBN 978-0-226-30879-1 (v. 1 : cloth : alk. paper) — ISBN 0-226-30879-0 (v. 1 : cloth : alk. paper) — ISBN 978-0-226-30880-7 (v. 1 : pbk. : alk. paper) — ISBN 0-226-30880-4 (v. 1 : pbk. : alk. paper) — ISBN 978-0-226-30934-7 (v. 1 : e-book) — ISBN 0-226-30934-7 (v. 1 : e-book) — ISBN 978-0-226-30877-7 (v. 2 : cloth : alk. paper) — ISBN 0-226-30877-4 (v. 2 : cloth : alk. paper) — ISBN 978-0-226-30878-4 (v. 2 : pbk. : alk. paper) — ISBN-10: 0-226-30878-2 (v. 2 : pbk. : alk. paper) —ISBN 978-0-226-30935-4 (v. 2 : e-book) — ISBN-10: 0-226-30935-5 (v. 2 : e-book) —ISBN 978-0-226-30881-4 (v. 3 : cloth : alk. paper) — ISBN 0-226-30881-2 (v. 3 : cloth : alk. paper) — ISBN 978-0-226-30882-1 (v. 3 : pbk. : alk. paper) — ISBN 0-226-30882-0 (v. 3 : pbk. : alk. paper) — ISBN 978-0-226-30936-1 (v. 3 : e-book) — ISBN 0-226-30936-3 (v. 3 : e-book)
  1. Euripides—Translations into English. 2. Mythology, Greek—Drama. I. Lattimore, Richmond Alexander, 1906–1984. II. Taplin, Oliver. III. Griffith, Mark, Ph. D. IV. Grene, David. V. Roberts, Deborah H. VI. Arrowsmith, William, 1924–1992. VII. Jones, Frank William Oliver, 1915– VIII. Vermeule, Emily. IX. Carson, Anne, 1950– X. Willetts, R. F. (Ronald Frederick), 1915–1999. XI. Euripides. Alcestis. English. XII. Title. XIII. Series: Complete Greek tragedies (Unnumbered)
  PA3975.A1 2012
  882'.01—dc23

2012015831

CONTENTS

EDITORS' PREFACE TO THE THIRD EDITION

The first edition of the *Complete Greek Tragedies*, edited by David Grene and Richmond Lattimore, was published by the University of Chicago Press starting in 1953. But the origins of the series go back even further. David Grene had already published his translation of three of the tragedies with the same press in 1942, and some of the other translations that eventually formed part of the Chicago series had appeared even earlier. A second edition of the series, with new translations of several plays and other changes, was published in 1991. For well over six decades, these translations have proved to be extraordinarily popular and resilient, thanks to their combination of accuracy, poetic immediacy, and clarity of presentation. They have guided hundreds of thousands of teachers, students, and other readers toward a reliable understanding of the surviving masterpieces of the three great Athenian tragedians: Aeschylus, Sophocles, and Euripides.

But the world changes, perhaps never more rapidly than in the past half century, and whatever outlasts the day of its appearance must eventually come to terms with circumstances very different from those that prevailed at its inception. During this same period, scholarly understanding of Greek tragedy has undergone significant development, and there have been marked changes not only in the readers to whom this series is addressed, but also in the ways in which these texts are taught and studied in universities. These changes have prompted the University of Chicago Press to perform another, more systematic revision of the translations, and we are honored to have been entrusted with this delicate and important task.

Our aim in this third edition has been to preserve and strengthen as far as possible all those features that have made the Chicago translations successful for such a long time, while at the same time revising the texts carefully and tactfully to bring them up to date and equipping them with various kinds of subsidiary help, so they may continue to serve new generations of readers.

Our revisions have addressed the following issues:

- Wherever possible, we have kept the existing translations. But we have revised them where we found this to be necessary in order to bring them closer to the ancient Greek of the original texts or to replace an English idiom that has by now become antiquated or obscure. At the same time we have done our utmost to respect the original translator's individual style and meter.
- In a few cases, we have decided to substitute entirely new translations for the ones that were published in earlier editions of the series. Euripides' *Medea* has been newly translated by Oliver Taplin, *The Children of Heracles* by Mark Griffith, *Andromache* by Deborah Roberts, and *Iphigenia among the Taurians* by Anne Carson. We have also, in the case of Aeschylus, added translations and brief discussions of the fragments of lost plays that originally belonged to connected tetralogies along with the surviving tragedies, since awareness of these other lost plays is often crucial to the interpretation of the surviving ones. And in the case of Sophocles, we have included a translation of the substantial fragmentary remains of one of his satyr-dramas, *The Trackers* (*Ichneutai*). (See "How the Plays Were Originally Staged" below for explanation of "tetralogy," "satyr-drama," and other terms.)
- We have altered the distribution of the plays among the various volumes in order to reflect the chronological order in which they were written, when this is known or can be estimated with some probability. Thus the *Oresteia* appears now as volume 2 of Aeschylus' tragedies, and the sequence of Euripides' plays has been rearranged.
- We have rewritten the stage directions to make them more consistent throughout, keeping in mind current scholarly under-

standing of how Greek tragedies were staged in the fifth century BCE. In general, we have refrained from extensive stage directions of an interpretive kind, since these are necessarily speculative and modern scholars often disagree greatly about them. The Greek manuscripts themselves contain no stage directions at all.

- We have indicated certain fundamental differences in the meters and modes of delivery of all the verse of these plays. Spoken language (a kind of heightened ordinary speech, usually in the iambic trimeter rhythm) in which the characters of tragedy regularly engage in dialogue and monologue is printed in ordinary Roman font; the sung verse of choral and individual lyric odes (using a large variety of different meters), and the chanted verse recited by the chorus or individual characters (always using the anapestic meter), are rendered in *italics*, with parentheses added where necessary to indicate whether the passage is sung or chanted. In this way, readers will be able to tell at a glance how the playwright intended a given passage to be delivered in the theater, and how these shifting dynamics of poetic register contribute to the overall dramatic effect.

- All the Greek tragedies that survive alternate scenes of action or dialogue, in which individual actors speak all the lines, with formal songs performed by the chorus. Occasionally individual characters sing formal songs too, or they and the chorus may alternate lyrics and spoken verse within the same scene. Most of the formal songs are structured as a series of pairs of stanzas of which the metrical form of the first one ("strophe") is repeated exactly by a second one ("antistrophe"). Thus the metrical structure will be, e.g., strophe A, antistrophe A, strophe B, antistrophe B, with each pair of stanzas consisting of a different sequence of rhythms. Occasionally a short stanza in a different metrical form ("mesode") is inserted in the middle between one strophe and the corresponding antistrophe, and sometimes the end of the whole series is marked with a single stanza in a different metrical form ("epode")—thus, e.g., strophe A, mesode, antistrophe A; or strophe A, antistrophe A, strophe B, antistrophe B, epode. We have indicated these metrical structures by inserting the terms

STROPHE, ANTISTROPHE, MESODE, and EPODE above the first line of the relevant stanzas so that readers can easily recognize the compositional structure of these songs.

- In each play we have indicated by the symbol ° those lines or words for which there are significant uncertainties regarding the transmitted text, and we have explained as simply as possible in textual notes at the end of the volume just what the nature and degree of those uncertainties are. These notes are not at all intended to provide anything like a full scholarly apparatus of textual variants, but instead to make readers aware of places where the text transmitted by the manuscripts may not exactly reflect the poet's own words, or where the interpretation of those words is seriously in doubt.

- For each play we have provided a brief introduction that gives essential information about the first production of the tragedy, the mythical or historical background of its plot, and its reception in antiquity and thereafter.

- For each of the three great tragedians we have provided an introduction to his life and work. It is reproduced at the beginning of each volume containing his tragedies.

- We have also provided at the end of each volume a glossary explaining the names of all persons and geographical features that are mentioned in any of the plays in that volume.

It is our hope that our work will help ensure that these translations continue to delight, to move, to astonish, to disturb, and to instruct many new readers in coming generations.

MARK GRIFFITH, *Berkeley*
GLENN W. MOST, *Florence*

INTRODUCTION
TO EURIPIDES

Little is known about the life of Euripides. He was probably born between 485 and 480 BCE on the island of Salamis near Athens. Of the three great writers of Athenian tragedy of the fifth century he was thus the youngest: Aeschylus was older by about forty years, Sophocles by ten or fifteen. Euripides is not reported to have ever engaged significantly in the political or military life of his city, unlike Aeschylus, who fought against the Persians at Marathon, and Sophocles, who was made a general during the Peloponnesian War. In 408 Euripides left Athens to go to the court of King Archelaus of Macedonia in Pella (we do not know exactly why). He died there in 406.

Ancient scholars knew of about ninety plays attributed to Euripides, and he was given permission to participate in the annual tragedy competition at the festival of Dionysus on twenty-two occasions—strong evidence of popular interest in his work. But he was not particularly successful at winning the first prize. Although he began competing in 455 (the year after Aeschylus died), he did not win first place until 441, and during his lifetime he received that award only four times; a fifth victory was bestowed on him posthumously for his trilogy *Iphigenia in Aulis, The Bacchae, Alcmaeon in Corinth* (this last play is lost), produced by one of his sons who was also named Euripides. By contrast, Aeschylus won thirteen victories and Sophocles eighteen. From various references, especially the frequent parodies of Euripides in the comedies of Aristophanes, we can surmise that many members of contemporary Athenian audiences objected to Euripides' tendency to make the characters of tragedy more modern and less heroic, to represent the passions of women, and to reflect recent developments in philosophy and music.

But in the centuries after his death, Euripides went on to become by far the most popular of the Greek tragedians. When the ancient Greeks use the phrase "the poet" without further specification and do not mean by it Homer, they always mean Euripides. Hundreds of fragments from his plays, mostly quite short, are found in quotations by other authors and in anthologies from the period between the third century BCE and the fourth century CE. Many more fragments of his plays have been preserved on papyrus starting in the fourth century BCE than of those by Aeschylus and Sophocles together, and far more scenes of his plays have been associated with images on ancient pottery starting in the same century and on frescoes in Pompeii and elsewhere and Roman sarcophagi some centuries later than is the case for either of his rivals. Some knowledge of his texts spread far and wide through collections of sententious aphorisms and excerpts of speeches and songs drawn from his plays (or invented in his name).

It was above all in the schools that Euripides became the most important author of tragedies: children throughout the Greek-speaking world learned the rules of language and comportment by studying first and foremost Homer and Euripides. But we know that Euripides' plays also continued to be performed in theaters for centuries, and the transmitted texts of some of the more popular ones (e.g., *Medea, Orestes*) seem to bear the traces of modifications by ancient producers and actors. Both in his specific plays and plots and in his general conception of dramatic action and character, Euripides massively influenced later Greek playwrights, not only tragic poets but also comic ones (especially Menander, the most important dramatist of New Comedy, born about a century and a half after Euripides)—and not only Greek ones, but Latin ones as well, such as Accius and Pacuvius, and later Seneca (who went on to exert a deep influence on Renaissance drama).

A more or less complete collection of his plays was made in

Alexandria during the third century BCE. Whereas, out of all the plays of Aeschylus and Sophocles, only seven tragedies each were chosen (no one knows by whom) at some point later in antiquity, probably in the second century CE, to represent their work, Euripides received the distinction of having ten plays selected as canonical: *Alcestis, Andromache, The Bacchae, Hecuba, Hippolytus, Medea, Orestes, The Phoenician Women, Rhesus* (scholars generally think this play was written by someone other than Euripides and was attributed to him in antiquity by mistake), and *The Trojan Women*. Of these ten tragedies, three—*Hecuba, Orestes,* and *The Phoenician Women*—were especially popular in the Middle Ages; they are referred to as the Byzantine triad, after the capital of the eastern Empire, Byzantium, known later as Constantinople and today as Istanbul.

The plays that did not form part of the selection gradually ceased to be copied, and thus most of them eventually were lost to posterity. We would possess only these ten plays and fragments of the others were it not for the lucky chance that a single volume of an ancient complete edition of Euripides' plays, arranged alphabetically, managed to survive into the Middle Ages. Thus we also have another nine tragedies (referred to as the alphabetic plays) whose titles in Greek all begin with the letters *epsilon, êta, iota,* and *kappa*: *Electra, Helen, The Children of Heracles* (*Hêrakleidai*), *Heracles, The Suppliants* (*Hiketides*), *Ion, Iphigenia in Aulis, Iphigenia among the Taurians,* and *The Cyclops* (*Kyklôps*). The Byzantine triad have very full ancient commentaries (scholia) and are transmitted by hundreds of medieval manuscripts; the other seven plays of the canonical selection have much sparser scholia and are transmitted by something more than a dozen manuscripts; the alphabetic plays have no scholia at all and are transmitted only by a single manuscript in rather poor condition and by its copies.

Modern scholars have been able to establish a fairly secure dating for most of Euripides' tragedies thanks to the exact indications provided by ancient scholarship for the first production of some of them and the relative chronology suggested by metrical and other features for the others. Accordingly the five volumes of this third edition have been organized according to the probable chronological sequence:

Volume 1: *Alcestis*: 438 BCE
           Medea: 431
           The Children of Heracles: ca. 430
           Hippolytus: 428
Volume 2: *Andromache*: ca. 425
           Hecuba: ca. 424
           The Suppliant Women: ca. 423
           Electra: ca. 420
Volume 3: *Heracles*: ca. 415
           The Trojan Women: 415
           Iphigenia among the Taurians: ca. 414
           Ion: ca. 413
Volume 4: *Helen*: 412
           The Phoenician Women: ca. 409
           Orestes: 408
Volume 5: *The Bacchae*: posthumously after 406
           Iphigenia in Aulis: posthumously after 406
           The Cyclops: date unknown
           Rhesus: probably spurious, from the fourth century BCE

In the Renaissance Euripides remained the most popular of the three tragedians. Directly and by the mediation of Seneca he influenced drama from the sixteenth to the eighteenth century far more than Aeschylus or Sophocles did. But toward the end of the eighteenth century and even more in the course of the nineteenth century, he came increasingly under attack yet again, as already in the fifth century BCE, and for much the same reason, as being decadent, tawdry, irreligious, and inharmonious. He was also criticized for his perceived departures from the ideal of "the tragic" (as exemplified by plays such as Sophocles' *Oedipus the King* and *Antigone*), especially in the "romance" plots of *Alcestis*,

Iphigenia among the Taurians, Ion, and *Helen.* It was left to the twentieth century to discover its own somewhat disturbing affinity to his tragic style and worldview. Nowadays among theatrical audiences, scholars, and nonprofessional readers Euripides is once again at least as popular as his two rivals.

HOW THE PLAYS WERE ORIGINALLY STAGED

Nearly all the plays composed by Aeschylus, Sophocles, and Euripides were first performed in the Theater of Dionysus at Athens, as part of the annual festival and competition in drama. This was not only a literary and musical event, but also an important religious and political ceremony for the Athenian community. Each year three tragedians were selected to compete, with each of them presenting four plays per day, a "tetralogy" of three tragedies and one satyr-play. The satyr-play was a type of drama similar to tragedy in being based on heroic myth and employing many of the same stylistic features, but distinguished by having a chorus of half-human, half-horse followers of Dionysus—sileni or satyrs—and by always ending happily. Extant examples of this genre are Euripides' *The Cyclops* (in *Euripides*, vol. 5) and Sophocles' *The Trackers* (partially preserved: in *Sophocles*, vol. 2).

The three competing tragedians were ranked by a panel of citizens functioning as amateur judges, and the winner received an honorific prize. Records of these competitions were maintained, allowing Aristotle and others later to compile lists of the dates when each of Aeschylus', Sophocles', and Euripides' plays were first performed and whether they placed first, second, or third in the competition (unfortunately we no longer possess the complete lists).

The tragedians competed on equal terms: each had at his disposal three actors (only two in Aeschylus' and in Euripides' earliest plays) who would often have to switch between roles as each play progressed, plus other nonspeaking actors to play attendants and other subsidiary characters; a chorus of twelve (in Aeschylus' time) or fifteen (for most of the careers of Sophocles and Euripides), who would sing and dance formal songs and whose Chorus Leader would engage in dialogue with the characters or offer comment on the action; and a pipe-player, to accompany the sung portions of the play.

All the performers were men, and the actors and chorus members all wore masks. The association of masks with other Dionysian rituals may have affected their use in the theater; but masks had certain practical advantages as well—for example, making it easy to play female characters and to change quickly between roles. In general, the use of masks also meant that ancient acting techniques must have been rather different from what we are used to seeing in the modern theater. Acting in a mask requires a more frontal and presentational style of performance toward the audience than is usual with unmasked, "realistic" acting; a masked actor must communicate far more by voice and stylized bodily gesture than by facial expression, and the gradual development of a character in the course of a play could hardly be indicated by changes in his or her mask. Unfortunately, however, we know almost nothing about the acting techniques of the Athenian theater. But we do know that the chorus members were all Athenian amateurs, and so were the actors up until the later part of the fifth century, by which point a prize for the best actor had been instituted in the tragic competition, and the art of acting (which of course included solo singing and dancing) was becoming increasingly professionalized.

The tragedian himself not only wrote the words for his play but also composed the music and choreography and directed the productions. It was said that Aeschylus also acted in his plays but that Sophocles chose not to, except early in his career, because his voice was too weak. Euripides is reported to have had a collaborator who specialized in musical composition. The costs for each playwright's production were shared between an individual wealthy citizen, as a kind of "super-tax" requirement, and the city.

The Theater of Dionysus itself during most of the fifth century BCE probably consisted of a large rectangular or trapezoidal dance floor, backed by a one-story wooden building (the *skênê*), with a large central door that opened onto the dance floor. (Some scholars have argued that two doors were used, but the evidence is thin.) Between the *skênê* and the dance floor there may have been a narrow stage on which the characters acted and which communicated easily with the dance floor. For any particular play, the *skênê* might represent a palace, a house, a temple, or a cave, for example; the interior of this "building" was generally invisible to the audience, with all the action staged in front of it. Sophocles is said to have been the first to use painted scenery; this must have been fairly simple and easy to remove, as every play had a different setting. Playwrights did not include stage directions in their texts. Instead, a play's setting was indicated explicitly by the speaking characters.

All the plays were performed in the open air and in daylight. Spectators sat on wooden seats in rows, probably arranged in rectangular blocks along the curving slope of the Acropolis. (The stone semicircular remains of the Theater of Dionysus that are visible today in Athens belong to a later era.) Seating capacity seems to have been four to six thousand—thus a mass audience, but not quite on the scale of the theaters that came to be built during the fourth century BCE and later at Epidaurus, Ephesus, and many other locations all over the Mediterranean.

Alongside the *skênê*, on each side, there were passages through which actors could enter and exit. The acting area included the dance floor, the doorway, and the area immediately in front of the *skênê*. Occasionally an actor appeared on the roof or above it, as if flying. He was actually hanging from a crane (*mêchanê*: hence *deus ex machina*, "a god from the machine"). The *skênê* was also occasionally opened up—the mechanical details are uncertain—in order to show the audience what was concealed within (usually dead bodies). Announcements of entrances and exits, like the setting, were made by the characters. Although the medieval manuscripts of the surviving plays do not provide explicit stage directions, it is usually possible to infer from the words or from the context whether a particular entrance or exit is being made through a door (into the *skênê*) or by one of the side entrances. In later antiquity, there may have been a rule that one side entrance always led to the city center, the other to the countryside or harbor. Whether such a rule was ever observed in the fifth century is uncertain.

HERACLES

Translated by WILLIAM ARROWSMITH

HERACLES: INTRODUCTION

The Play: Date and Composition

It is not certain when Euripides' *Heracles* was first produced, but metrical considerations suggest a date of around 415 BCE. Presumably Euripides wrote it for the annual competition at the Great Dionysian Festival in Athens. What the other three plays were in Euripides' tetralogy of that year, and how they fared in the dramatic competition, are unknown.

The play is sometimes referred to with a Latin title (derived from a tragedy by Seneca), *Hercules furens* ("Hercules Insane"). Presumably Euripides originally titled it simply *Heracles*, and the further specification was added when it was included in a complete edition of his works (perhaps around the third century BCE) in order to distinguish it from his other plays about Heracles.

The Myth

Heracles, son of Zeus and Alcmene (the wife of Amphitryon), was one of the greatest and most popular heroes throughout the ancient world, a symbol of unconquerably robust masculine vitality and courage. But during his whole life he was harassed by the fierce opposition of the goddess Hera; and the very same uncontrollable strength that enabled him to achieve celebrated triumphs over monsters, criminals, and other enemies of mankind also sometimes led to his committing dreadful excesses and crimes himself. It is this paradoxical combination of heroic greatness and terrible destructiveness that Euripides explores in *Heracles*.

At the beginning of the play, Heracles is away in the under-world performing one of his impossible labors, to bring Hades' monstrous guard dog Cerberus up to the light of day. In the meantime, in Thebes, Heracles' wife Megara and their sons are being threatened with death by the usurping king of the city, Lycus. Heracles returns in the nick of time to kill Lycus and rescue his family. All seems to have ended well; but suddenly Hera drives him temporarily mad by means of her minions, Madness and Iris, and in his insanity he kills his wife and all his children. When Heracles comes to himself again and recognizes what he has done, he decides to commit suicide; but then Theseus, the king of Athens, unexpectedly arrives, offers him understanding and friendship, and persuades him to remain alive and to come with him to Athens, where he will receive honors.

The general image of Heracles both as a civilizing culture hero and as author of terrible crimes is fundamental to this play and was already very familiar in Euripides' time. Moreover, the story of Heracles' madness had been recounted in different versions by a number of older epic and lyric poets and by at least one recent prose author, Pherecydes of Athens. So Euripides' audience was not likely to have been surprised by some basic aspects of the play. But Euripides also seems to have made three specific innovations in the plot: (1) the figure of the usurper Lycus, whose transparent name ("Wolf") and detailed introduction when he is first mentioned suggest that Euripides may well have invented him (though an earlier Lycus, ancestor or father of this one, was an established figure in Theban mythology); (2) the sequence according to which Heracles murders his children (and also, unusually, his wife Megara) only after he has successfully concluded his labors (perhaps in the original sequence Heracles' labors were his punishment for murdering his sons); and (3) the insertion of Theseus into the story with his offer to Heracles of honors in Athens. These innovations serve to create a series of astonishing reversals of fortune and to focus the spectators' attention both upon the nature of true courage and upon the paradoxical relations between heroism and violence, between grandeur and misery, between men and women and children, and perhaps above all between the cruelty of the gods and the friendship of humans.

Transmission and Reception

Heracles survived antiquity only by the accident of being among the so-called "alphabetic plays" (see "Introduction to Euripides," p. 3), and it is transmitted only by a single manuscript (and its copies). It is not accompanied by ancient commentaries (scholia) that explain various kinds of interpretative difficulties. But evidence that it achieved at least a limited degree of popularity in antiquity is provided by the fact that a couple of ancient papyri bearing parts of its text have been discovered.

The story of Heracles' madness was told by various ancient Greek and Latin authors in texts now lost which may well have been inspired by Euripides, and it seems to have left some traces, though not many, in ancient art. But it was the Roman philosopher and tragedian Seneca's *Hercules furens* that made the story celebrated in world literature, overshadowing until recently Euripides' version. While Seneca's play certainly derives at least in part directly from Euripides' tragedy, scholars disagree on whether Seneca also made use of other versions of the story which might themselves have been ultimately inspired by Euripides.

In modern times *Heracles* has never been among Euripides' most popular plays and has not often been staged. In the Renaissance, Seneca's version of the story was much more influential, and for centuries it provided a compelling model for dramatizing madness. But since the late nineteenth century Euripides' play has moved out from the shadow of Seneca's and has inspired a dramatic monologue by Robert Browning (*Aristophanes' Apology*, 1875) and verse dramas, all titled *Herakles*, by George Cabot Lodge (1908), Frank Wedekind (1917), Archibald MacLeish (1967), and Heiner Müller (1975). Scholars used to be perplexed by the play's two-part construction—a dramatic structure found in many of Euripides' plays—and went to great trouble to find in it elements of overarching dramatic, thematic, and psychological unity. But nowadays its depiction of humans trapped in a chillingly arbitrary and hostile world and sustained only by their love and loyalty for one another strikes many readers as particularly timely and moving.

HERACLES

Characters   AMPHITRYON, father of Heracles
                 MEGARA, wife of Heracles
                 CHORUS of old men of Thebes
                 LYCUS, usurper of the throne of Thebes
                 HERACLES, hero of Thebes
                 IRIS, messenger of the gods
                 MADNESS
                 MESSENGER
                 THESEUS, king of Athens

*Scene: In front of the palace of Heracles at Thebes. In the foreground
is the altar of Zeus the Savior. Amphitryon, Megara, and her three
small sons sit on it as suppliants.*

AMPHITRYON
     What mortal lives who has not heard this name—
     Amphitryon of Argos, who shared his wife
     with Zeus? I am he: son of Alcaeus
     Perseus' son, and father of Heracles.
     Here I settled, in this Thebes, where once the earth   5
     was sown with dragon teeth and sprouted men;
     and Ares saved but few, that they might people
     Cadmus' city with their children's children.
     From these Sown Men Creon was descended,
     son of Menoeceus and our late king.
     This lady is Megara, Creon's daughter,
     for whose wedding once all Thebes shrilled   10

to pipes and songs as she was led, a bride,
home to my halls by famous Heracles.
Then my son left home, Thebes, left Megara and kin,
hoping to recover the plain of Argos
and those gigantic walls from which I fled   15
to Thebes, because I killed Electryon.
He hoped to win me back my native land
and so alleviate my grief. And therefore,
mastered by Hera's goads or by his fate,
he promised to Eurystheus a vast price
for our return: to civilize the world.   20
When all his other labors had been done,
he undertook the last: descended down
to Hades through the jaws of Taenarus
to hale back up to the light of day
the triple-bodied dog.

                    He has not come back.   25
     Here in Thebes an ancient legend goes
that once a certain Lycus married Dirce
and ruled this city with its seven gates
before the twins of Zeus, those "white colts,"
Amphion and Zethus, ruled the land.   30
This Lycus' namesake and descendant,
no native Theban but Euboean-born,
attacked our city, sick with civil war,
murdered Creon and usurped his throne.
And now our marriage bond with Creon's house   35
has proved in fact to be our greatest ill.
For since my son is gone beneath the earth,
this land's new tyrant, Lycus, plans to kill
the sons and wife of Heracles—and me,
so old and useless, that I scarcely count—   40
blotting murder with murder, lest these boys,
grown to men, someday revenge their mother's kin.

     My son, when he descended to the darkness
underground, left me here, appointing me

both nurse and guardian of his little sons. 45
Now, to keep these heirs of Heracles from death,
I have set them and their mother in supplication
upon this altar to Zeus the Savior,
established by my noble son, a trophy
for the victory of his spear over the Minyans. 50
Here we sit, in utter destitution,
lacking food, water, and clothing; having no beds
but the bare earth beneath our bodies; sitting
barred from our house, no hope of being rescued.
And of our friends, some prove no friends at all, 55
while those still true are powerless to help.
This is what misfortune means among mankind;
upon no man who wished me well at all,
could I wish this acid test of friends might come.

MEGARA
Old man, marshal of our famous Theban arms, 60
who once destroyed the city of the Taphians,
how dark are all the ways of gods to man!
Prosperity was my inheritance:
I had a father who could boast of wealth,
who was a king—such power as makes the long spears 65
leap with greed against its proud possessor—
a father, blessed with children, who gave me
in glorious marriage to your Heracles.
But now his glory has died and taken wing
and you and I, old man, shall soon be dead, 70
and with us, these small sons of Heracles
whom I ward and nestle underwing like fledglings.
First one, and then another, questions me,
and asks: "Mother, where has Father gone?
What is he doing? When will he come back?"
Then, too small to understand, they ask again 75
for "Father." I put them off with stories;
but when the hinges creak, they all leap up

to run and throw themselves at their father's feet.
Now is there any hope? What means of rescue
do we have, old man? I look to you.   80
The border is impassable by stealth;
strong sentries have been set on every road;
all hope that friends might rescue us is gone.
So tell me now if you have any plan,   85
for otherwise it's certain we shall die.

AMPHITRYON

My child, I find it hard in such a case
to give advice offhand without hard thought.
We are weak and, being weak, should play for time.°

MEGARA

Wait for worse? Do you love life so much?   90

AMPHITRYON

I love it even now. I love its hopes.

MEGARA

And I. But hope is of things possible.

AMPHITRYON

A cure may come in wearing out the time.

MEGARA

It is the time between that tortures me.

AMPHITRYON

Even now, out of our very evils,   95
for you and me a better wind may blow.
My son, your husband, still may come. Be calm;
dry the living springs of tears that fill
your children's eyes. Console them with stories,
those sweet thieves of wretched make-believe.   100
Human misery must somewhere have a stop:
there is no wind that always blows a storm;
great good fortune comes to failure in the end.
All is change; all yields its place and goes;

to persevere, trusting in what hopes he has,   105
is courage in a man. The coward despairs.

(Enter the Chorus of old men of Thebes from the side.)

CHORUS [*singing*]

STROPHE

Leaning on our staffs we come
to the vaulted halls and the old man's bed,
our song the dirge of the dying swan,   110
ourselves mere words, ghosts that walk
in the visions of night,
trembling with age,
but eager to help.
O children, fatherless sons,
old man and wretched wife   115
who mourn your lord in Hades!

ANTISTROPHE

Do not falter. Drag your weary feet°
onward like the colt that, yoked and straining,   120
tugs uphill, on rock, the heavy chariot.
If any man should stumble,
grab his hands and clothing;
age, support his aged years   125
as once when you were young
he supported you, his peers
in the toils of war
and you all were no blot on your country's fame.

EPODE

Look how the children's eyes   130
flash forth like their father's!
His misfortune has not left them,
nor his loveliness.
O Hellas, Hellas,
losing these boys,   135
what allies you lose!

(Enter Lycus from the side.)

CHORUS LEADER
No more. Look: I see my country's tyrant,
Lycus, approaching the palace.

LYCUS
                                                You there,
father of Heracles, and you, his wife: 140
allow me one question. And you must allow it:
I am the power here; I ask what I wish.
How long will you seek to prolong your lives?
What hope have you? What could prevent your death?
Or do you think the father of these boys   145
who lies dead in Hades will still come back?
How much you exaggerate in mourning for your deaths—
you who filled all Hellas with your silly boasts
that Zeus was partner in your son's conception;
and you, that you were wife of the noblest man!   150
What was so prodigious in your husband's deeds?
Because he killed a Hydra in a marsh?
Or the Nemean lion? They were trapped in nets,
not strangled, as he claims, with his bare hands.
Are these your arguments? Because of this,   155
you say, the sons of Heracles should live—
a man who, coward in everything else,
made his reputation fighting beasts,
who never buckled shield upon his arm,
never came near a spear, but held a bow,   160
the coward's weapon, ready to run away?
The bow is no proof of manly courage;
no, your real man stands firm in the ranks
and dares to face the gash the spear may make.
          My policy, old man, is not mere cruelty;   165
call it caution. I am well aware
that I killed Creon, the father of this woman,
and only on this basis rule this land.

It does not suit my wishes that these boys
grow up to take their own revenge on me.

AMPHITRYON
Let Zeus defend his interest in his son.   170
For my part, Heracles, I'll have to argue,
and prove this man's gross ignorance of you:
I cannot bear that you should be abused.
First for that slander (for such I call it
when you are called a coward, Heracles).   175
I call upon the gods to bear me witness:
that thunder of Zeus, that chariot in which
Heracles rode, piercing with winged shafts
the breasts of those giants spawned by earth,
and raised the victory cry with the gods!   180
Go to Pholoë, you coward king, and ask
the Centaurs, those four-legged monsters,
what man they judge to be the bravest,
if not my son, whose courage you call sham.
Go ask Abantian Dirphys which raised you: 185
it will not praise you. You have never done
one brave deed your fatherland could cite.
You sneer at that wise invention, the bow.
Listen to me and learn what wisdom is.
Your spearman is the slave of his weapons: 190
unless his comrades in the ranks fight well,°
then he dies, killed by their cowardice;
and if his spear, his sole defense, is smashed,
he has no means of warding death away.
But the man whose hands know how to aim the bow,   195
holds the one best weapon: a thousand arrows shot,
he still has more to guard himself from death.
He stands far off, shooting at foes who see
only the wound the unseen arrow plows,
while he himself, his body unexposed,   200
lies screened and safe. This is best in war:

to preserve yourself and to hurt your foe
without relying overmuch on chance.
Such are my arguments, squarely opposed
to yours on every point at issue here.
What will you achieve by killing these boys?   205
How have they hurt you? Yet I grant you wise
in one respect: being base yourself,
you fear the children of a noble man.
Still, this goes hard with us, that we must die
because of your cowardice—a fate which you   210
might better suffer at our better hands,
if the mind of Zeus intended justice here.
But if the scepter is what you desire,
then let us go as exiles from the land.
But beware of force, lest you suffer it,   215
when the veering wind of god swings round again.
        O country of Cadmus, on you too
my reproaches fall! Is this then your help
for the sons of Heracles? For Heracles,
who single-handed fought your Minyan foe   220
and made Thebes see once more with free men's eyes?
No more can I praise Hellas, nor be still,
finding her so craven toward my son:
with fire, spears, and armor she should have come
to help these boys in gratitude to him,   225
for all his labors clearing land and sea.
Poor children, both Thebes and Hellas fail you.
And so you turn to me, a weak old man,
nothing more now than a jawing of words,
forsaken by that strength I used to have,   230
left only with this trembling husk of age.
But if my youth and strength could come again,
I'd take my spear and bloody your blond hair
until you ran beyond the bounds of Atlas,
trying, coward, to outrun my spear!   235

CHORUS LEADER

Don't brave men always find good things to say?
They never fail, although their tongue be slow.

LYCUS

Go on, rant, pile up your tower of words!
My actions, not my words, shall answer your abuse.

(To his servants.)

Go, some of you, to Helicon, others to Parnassus: 240
tell the woodsmen there to chop up oaken logs
and haul them to the city. Then pile your wood
around the altar here on every side,
and let it blaze. Burn them all alive
until they learn the dead man rules no more;   245
I, and I alone, am the power here.

(Some of Lycus' servants exit to the side.)

But you old men, for this defiance of yours,
you shall mourn not only the sons of Heracles
but also troubles that will afflict your homes,   250
as each one suffers something, until you learn
that you are only slaves; I am the master.

CHORUS LEADER°   *(To the Chorus.)*

O sons of earth, men whom Ares sowed,
teeth he tore from the dragon's savage jaw,
up, up with these staffs that prop our arms
and batter the skull of this godless man,   255
no Theban, but an alien lording it
over our citizens,° to our great shame!

(To Lycus.)

Never shall you boast that I am your slave,
never will you reap the harvest of my work,
all I labored for. Go back whence you came;   260

rage there. So long as there is life in me,
you shall not kill the sons of Heracles.
He has not gone so deep beneath the earth.
Because you ruined, then usurped, this land,
he who gave it help is going without his due.   265
Am I a meddler, then, because I help
the friend who, being dead, needs help the most?
O right hand, how you ache to hold a spear,
but cannot—your desire founders on your weakness.
Else, I would have stopped your mouth that calls me slave,   270
and helped this Thebes, in which you now exult,
to my credit. But corrupt with evil schemes
and civil strife, this city lost its mind;
for were it sane, it would not live your slave.

MEGARA

Old sirs, I thank you. Friends rightly show   275
just indignation on their friends' behalf.
But do not let your rage on our account
involve your ruin too. Amphitryon,
hear what I think for what it may be worth.
I love my children. How not love these boys   280
born of my labors? And I think that death
is terrible. And yet how base a thing it is
when a man will struggle with necessity!
We have to die. Then do we have to die
being burned alive, mocked by those we hate?—   285
for me a worse disaster than to die.
Our house and birth demand a better death.
Upon your helm the victor's glory sits,
forbidding that you die a coward's death;
while my husband needs no witnesses to swear   290
he would not want these sons of his to live
as cowards in men's eyes. Disgrace that hurts
his sons will break a man of noble birth;

and I must imitate my husband here.
Consider of what stuff your hopes are made.   295
You think your son will come from underground?
Who of all the dead comes home from Hades?
Or do you think we'll mellow Lycus with prayers?
No, you must shun a stupid enemy;
yield to noble, understanding men   300
who, met halfway as friends, will compromise.
The thought had come to me that prayers might win
the children's banishment; but this is worse,
to preserve them for a life of beggary.
How does the saying go? Hardly one day   305
do men look kindly on their banished friend.
Dare death with us, which awaits you anyway.
By your great soul, I challenge you, old friend.
The man who struggles hard against his fate
shows spirit, but the spirit of a fool.   310
No man alive can budge necessity.

CHORUS LEADER
I would have stopped the mouth of any man
who threatened you, had I my old strength back.
But now I am nothing. With you it rests,
Amphitryon, to avert disaster now.   315

AMPHITRYON
Not cowardice, not love of life, keeps me
from death, but my hope to save these children.
I am in love, it seems, with what cannot be.

                                                              (To Lycus.)

Here, king, here is my throat, ready for your sword;
murder me, stab me through, hurl me from a cliff,   320
but, grant, my lord, to Megara and me just this:
murder us before you kill these children;
spare us from seeing that ghastly sight,

these boys gasping out their lives, crying
"Mother!" and "Grandfather!" For the rest,   325
do your worst. Our hope is gone; we have to die.

MEGARA

And I beg you, grant me this one request,
and so by one act you shall oblige us both.
Let me adorn my children for their death;
open those doors which are locked to us   330
and give them that much share of their father's house.

LYCUS

I grant it. Attendants, undo the bolts!

(Lycus' servants open the door of the palace.)

Go in and dress. I do not begrudge you clothes.
But when your dressing for your death is done,
then I shall give you to the world below.   335

(Exit Lycus to the side.)

MEGARA

Come, my sons, follow your poor mother's steps
into your father's halls. Other men
possess his wealth; we just possess his name.

(Exit Megara with her children into the palace.)

AMPHITRYON

For nothing, then, O Zeus, you shared my wife!
In vain we called you partner in my son!   340
Your love then was much less than we had thought;
and I, mere man, am nobler than you, great god—
I did not betray the sons of Heracles.
You know well enough to creep into a bed
and take what is not yours, what no man gave: 345
what do you know of saving those you love?
You are a foolish god or were born unjust!

(Exit Amphitryon into the palace.)

CHORUS [*singing*]

STROPHE A

First for joy, the victor's song;
then the dirge; sing ailinos for Linos!
So Apollo sings, sweeping with golden pick   350
his lyre of lovely voice.
And so I sing of him
who went in darkness underground—
be he the son of Zeus,
be he Amphitryon's—
of him I sing, a dirge of praise,   355
a crown of song upon his labors.
For of noble deeds the praises are
    the glory of the dead.

MESODE A

First he cleared the grove of Zeus,
and slew the lion in its lair;   360
the tawny hide concealed his back,
oval of those dreadful jaws
    cowled his golden hair.

ANTISTROPHE A

Next the Centaurs: slaughtered them,
that mountain-ranging savage race,   365
laid them low with murderous shafts,
with winged arrows slew them all.
Too well the land had known them:
Peneus' lovely rapids,
vast plains, unharvested,
homesteads under Pelion,   370
and the places near Homole,
whence their cavalry rode forth
with pine-tree weapons,
    and ruled all Thessaly.

And next he slew the spotted deer 375
whose head grew with golden antlers,
that robber-beast, that ravager,
whose hide now gilds Oenoë's shrine,
　　　for Artemis the huntress.

STROPHE B

Then mounted to his car 380
and mastered with the bit
Diomedes' mares, that knew
no bridle, stabled in blood,
greedy jaws champing flesh,
foul mares that fed on men! 385
And thence crossed over
swirling silver, Hebrus' waters,
on and on, performing labors
　　　for Mycenae's king.

MESODE B

And there by Pelion's headland,
near the waters of Anaurus, 390
his shafts brought Cycnus down,
that stranger-slaying monster,
　　　crude dweller in Amphanae.

ANTISTROPHE B

Thence among the singing maidens,
western halls' Hesperides, 395
plucked by hand among the leaves
the golden fruit, and slew
the orchard's dragon guard
whose tail of amber coiled the trunk
untouchably. He passed beyond the sea 400
and set calm sailing in the lives of men
　　　whose living is the oar.

Under bellied heaven next,
he put his hands as props:
there in the halls of Atlas,   405
his manly strength held up
      heaven's starry halls.

STROPHE C

He passed the swelling sea of black,
and fought the Amazonian force
foregathered at Maeotis   410
where the many rivers meet.
What town of Hellas missed him
as he mustered friends to fight,
to win the warrior women's
gold-encrusted robes, in quest
for a girdle's deadly quarry?   415
And Hellas won the prize, spoils
of a famous barbarian queen,
      which now Mycenae keeps.

MESODE C

He seared each deadly Hydra-head   420
of Lerna's thousand-headed hound;
in her venom dipped the shaft
that brought three-bodied Geryon down,
      herdsman of Erytheia.

ANTISTROPHE C

And many races more he ran,
and won in all the victor's crown,   425
whose harbor now is Hades' tears,
the final labor of them all;
there his life is disembarked
in grief. He comes no more.
His friends have left his house,   430

and Charon's ferry waits
to take his children's lives
on the godless, lawless trip of no return.
To your hands your house still turns,
  but you are gone! 435

EPODE C

Could I have my youth once more,
could I shake my spear once more
beside the comrades of my youth,
my courage now would champion
your sons. But youth comes back no more 440
  that blessed me once.

   (Enter Megara, the children, and Amphitryon from the
    palace, dressed in the garments of the dead.)

CHORUS [*now chanting*]
 Look: I see the children coming now,
 wearing the garments of the grave,
 sons of Heracles who once was great;
 and there, his wife, drawing her sons 445
 behind her as she comes; and the old man,
 father of Heracles. O pitiful sight!
 I cannot stop the tears that break
  from these old eyes. 450

MEGARA
 Where is the priest with sacrificial knife?
 Where is the killer of our wretched lives?°
 Here the victims stand, ready for Hades.
 O my boys, this incongruity of death:
 beneath one yoke, old men, children, and mothers. 455
 How miserably we die, these children and I!
 Upon these faces now I look my last.
 I gave you birth and brought you up to be
 but mocked and murdered by our enemies.

Ah!

How bitterly my hopes for you have failed,   460
those hopes I founded on your father's words.

(To each child in turn.)

To you your father would have left all Argos:
in Eurystheus' halls you would have ruled
and held the sway over rich Pelasgia.
It was upon your head he sometimes threw   465
the skin of tawny lion that he wore.
You, made king of chariot-loving Thebes,
would have inherited your mother's lands,
because your coaxing won them from your father.
Sometimes in play, he put in your right hand   470
that carven club he kept for self-defense.
To you, he would have left Oechalia,
ravaged once by his far-shooting shafts.
There are three of you, and with three kingdoms
your heroic father raised you up on high.   475
And I was choosing each of you a bride,
from Athens, Thebes, and Sparta, binding our house
by marriage, that having such strong anchors down,
you might in happiness ride out your lives.
Now all is gone, and fortune, veering round,   480
gives each of you your death as though a bride,
and in my tears your bridal shower is,
while your father's father hosts the wedding feast
that makes you all the sons-in-law of death.
Which shall I take first, which of you the last,   485
to lift you up, take in my arms and kiss?
If only I could gather up my tears,
and like the tawny bee from every flower,
distill to one small nectar all my grief!
O dearest Heracles, if any voice   490
of mortals reaches Hades, hear me now!

Your sons, your father, are dying . . . and I,
who was once called blessed because of you.
Help us, come! Come, even as a ghost;
even as a dream, your coming would suffice.   495
For these are cowards who destroy your sons.

AMPHITRYON
Send on your prayers, my child, to those below,
while I hold out my hands and call to heaven.
We implore you, Zeus, if still you mean to help,
help us now before it is too late.   500
How often have I called! In vain, my labors.
For death is on us like necessity.
          Our lives, old friends, are but a little thing,
so let them run as sweetly as you can,
and give no thought to grief from day to night.
For time is not concerned to save our hopes,   505
but hurries on its business, and is gone.
You see in me a man who once had fame,
who did great deeds; but fortune in one day
has snatched it from me as though it were a feather.   510
Great wealth, great reputation! I know no man
with whom they stay. Friends of my youth, farewell.
You look your last on him who loved you well.

                              (*Enter Heracles from the side.*)

MEGARA
Look, Father! Is that my beloved? Can it be?

AMPHITRYON
I cannot say. I dare not say, my child.   515

MEGARA
It is he, whom we heard was beneath the earth,
unless some dream comes walking in the light.
A dream? This is no dream my longing makes!
It is he indeed, old man, your son, no other!

Run, children, hold tight to your father's robes   520
and never let him go! Quick, run! He comes
to rescue us and Zeus comes with him.

HERACLES

I greet my hearth! I hail my house and halls!
How gladly I behold the light once more
and look on you!   525
                              But what is this I see?
My children before the house? With funeral garlands
set on their heads? And here my wife surrounded
by a crowd of men? My father in tears?
What misfortune makes him cry? I'll go and ask
what disaster now has come upon my house.   530

MEGARA°

O my dearest . . .

AMPHITRYON

                              O daylight returning!

MEGARA

You come, alive, in time to rescue us!

HERACLES

Father, what's happened? What trouble does this mean?

MEGARA

Murder. Forgive me, Father, if I snatch
and speak the words that you should rightly say.   535
I am a woman: anguish hurts me more,
and my children were being put to death, and I.

HERACLES

Apollo! What a prelude to your tale!

MEGARA

My aged father is dead. My brothers too.

HERACLES

What! How did they die? Who killed them?   540

MEGARA

Murdered by Lycus, new tyrant of this land.

HERACLES

In open warfare? Or in civil strife?

MEGARA

In civil war. Now he rules our seven gates.

HERACLES

But why should you and my father be afraid?

MEGARA

He planned to kill us: your sons, father, and me.   545

HERACLES

What had he to fear from my orphaned sons?

MEGARA

Lest they take revenge some day for Creon's death.

HERACLES

But why these garments? Why are they dressed for death?

MEGARA

It was for our own deaths we put them on.

HERACLES

You would have died by violence? O gods!   550

MEGARA

We had no friends. We heard that you were dead.

HERACLES

How did you come to give up hope for me?

MEGARA

The heralds of Eurystheus proclaimed you dead.

HERACLES

Why did you abandon my house and hearth?

MEGARA

By force. He dragged your father from his bed.   555

HERACLES

He had no shame, but so dishonored age?

MEGARA

Lycus have shame? He knows of no such goddess.

HERACLES

And were my friends so scarce when I was gone?

MEGARA

In misfortune, what friend remains a friend?

HERACLES

They thought so little of my Minyan wars?   560

MEGARA

Again I say, misfortune has no friends.

HERACLES

Rip from your heads those wreaths of Hades!
Lift your faces to the light; with seeing eyes,
take your sweet reprieve from death and darkness.
And I—a task for my own hand alone—   565
shall go and raze this upstart tyrant's house,
cut off that blaspheming head and give it
to the dogs to feast on. All those men of Thebes
who took my goodness and returned me ill—
these arms with which I won the victor's crown   570
shall slaughter them, with rain of wingèd shafts
till all Ismenus chokes upon the corpses
and Dirce's silver waters run with blood.
Whom should I defend if not my wife and sons
and my old father? Farewell, my labors!   575
For wrongly I preferred you to these here.
They would have died for me, so I'll risk death
in their defense. Or is this bravery,

to do Eurystheus' orders and contend
with lions and Hydras, and not to struggle   580
for my children's lives? If so, from this time forth,
call me no more "Heracles the victor."

CHORUS LEADER
This is right, that a man defend his sons,
his aged father, and his wedded wife.

AMPHITRYON
My son, it is like you to love your friends   585
and hate your foe. But do not act too fast.

HERACLES
How do I act faster than I should?

AMPHITRYON
The king has henchmen, a mob of needy men°
who pass themselves off for men of wealth.
These men, their substance drained away by sloth   590
and spending, have promoted civil strife
and wrecked the state to plunder from their neighbors.
You were seen coming here. Beware therefore
lest your enemy be stronger than you guess.

HERACLES
I do not care if all the city saw me!   595
But seeing a bird in some foreboding place,
I guessed some trouble had fallen on my house,
and thus forewarned, I entered secretly.

AMPHITRYON
Good. Go now, enter your house and greet your hearth.
Look on your father's house; let it behold you.   600
Shortly the king will come to hale us off
and slaughter us: your wife, your sons, and me.
Wait here, and everything shall come to hand,
with safety too. But let the city go,
my son, until you finish matters here.   605

HERACLES

You advise me well. I will go within.
I owe first greetings to my household gods
because I have come home from sunless caves
of Kore and Hades. I shall not slight them.

AMPHITRYON

Did you really descend to Hades, son?   610

HERACLES

Yes; I brought back the triple-headed dog.

AMPHITRYON

You subdued him? or was he the goddess' gift?

HERACLES

Subdued him. Luck was mine: I had seen the Mysteries.

AMPHITRYON

And is the monster at Eurystheus' house?

HERACLES

No, at Hermione, in Demeter's grove.   615

AMPHITRYON

Does Eurystheus know of your return above?

HERACLES

No, I came here first to learn of you.

AMPHITRYON

Why did you delay so long underground?

HERACLES

I lingered to rescue Theseus from Hades.

AMPHITRYON

Where is he now? Gone to his native land?   620

HERACLES

He went to Athens, rejoicing to be free.

(To his children.)

Follow your father to the house, my sons,
for this, your going in, shall be more fair
than your coming out. Put your fears away,
and stop those tears that well up in your eyes.   625
And you, dear wife, gather your courage up,
tremble no more, and let my garments go.
I have no wings to fly from those I love.
Look:
They will not let me go, but clutch my clothes
more tightly still. Were you so close to death?   630
Here, I'll take your hands and lead you in my wake,
like a ship that tows its cargo boats behind,
for I accept this care and service
of my sons. Here all mankind is equal:
rich and poor alike, they love their children.
With wealth distinctions come: some possess it,   635
some do not. But all mankind loves its children.

                    (Exit Heracles with the children, Megara,
                        and Amphitryon, into the palace.)

CHORUS [singing]
                    STROPHE A
Youth I long for always.
But old age lies on my head,
a weight more heavy than Aetna's rocks;
darkness hides   640
the light from my eyes.
Had I the wealth of an Asian king,
or a palace crammed with gold,   645
both would I give for youth,
loveliest in wealth,
in poverty, loveliest.
But old age I loathe: ugly,
murderous. Let the waves take it   650
so it comes no more to the homes

and cities of men! Let the wind
  whirl it away forever!

If the gods were wise and understood men,   655
second youth would be their gift,
to seal the virtue of a man.
And so the good would run their course   660
from death back to the light again.
But evil men should live their lap,
one single life, and run no more.
By such a sign all men would know
the wicked from the good,   665
as when the clouds are broken
and the sailor sees the stars.
But now the gods have set
between the noble and the base
no clear distinction down.   670
And time and age go wheeling on,
  exalting only wealth.

Never shall I cease from this,
Muses with the Graces joining,
loveliness in yoke together.   675
May I not live without the Muses!
Let my head be always crowned!
May my old age always sing
of Memory, the Muses' mother!
Always shall I sing the crown   680
of Heracles the victor!
So long as these remain—
    Dionysus' gift of wine,
    the lyre of seven strings,
    the shrilling of the pipe—
never shall I cease to sing,   685
    Muses who made me dance!

Paeans sing the Delian maidens,
a song for Leto's lovely son,
wheeling at the temple gates
the lovely mazes of the dance.   690
So paeans at your gate I'll raise,
pouring like the dying swan,
from hoary throat a song of praise.
I have a noble theme of song: 695
He is the son of Zeus!
But far beyond his birth,
his courage° lifts him up,
whose labors gave to mortals calm,
who cleared away the beasts.   700

(Enter Lycus from the side, and Amphitryon from the palace.)

LYCUS

None too soon, Amphitryon, have you appeared.
A long time now you all have spent in dallying
with your robes and ornaments of death.
Go, call the wife and sons of Heracles
and bid them show themselves before the house   705
according to your promise to die freely.

AMPHITRYON

King, you persecute in me a wretched man,
and by abusing us, you wrong the dead.
King you may be, but tread more gently here.
Death is your decree, and we accept it   710
as we must. As you decide, then so must we.

LYCUS

Where is Megara? Where are Heracles' children?

AMPHITRYON

To chance a guess from here outside, I think . . .

LYCUS

Well, what do you think? What is your evidence?

AMPHITRYON

. . . she is kneeling at the hearth and makes her prayers . . .   715

LYCUS

If she asks for life, her prayers are pointless.

AMPHITRYON

. . . and implores in vain her perished husband to come.

LYCUS

He is not here to help. He will not come.

AMPHITRYON

Not unless some god restore him to us.

LYCUS

Go inside and fetch her from the house.   720

AMPHITRYON

Then I would be accomplice in her death.

LYCUS

Very well then. Since your scruples forbid,
I, who lack such petty fears, shall go and fetch
the mother and her sons. Attend me, guards,
and help me put good riddance to this chore.   725

(Exit Lycus, attended by guards, into the palace.)

AMPHITRYON

Go, march in to your fate. Someone, I think,
will do the rest. Expect for what you did
evil in return. How justly, old friends,
into that net whose meshes hide the sword,
he goes, the man who would have slaughtered us,   730
coward that he is! I'll go in and watch
his body fall. This is sweet: to see your foe
perish and pay to justice all he owes.

(Exit Amphitryon into the palace.)

CHORUS [*singing in this interchange, while the Chorus Leader and Lycus
speak in reply*]

STROPHE A

> *Disaster is reversed!*
> *Our great king's life returns from Hades!* 735
> *Justice flows back! O fate of the gods,*
> *returning!*

CHORUS LEADER

> Your time has come. You go now where the price 740
> for outrage on your betters must be paid.

CHORUS

> *Joy once more! I weep for joy!*
> *The king has come again!*
> *He has come, of whom I had no hope,* 745
> *my country's king, come back again!*

CHORUS LEADER

> Let's look within the house, old friends. Let's see
> if someone is doing as I hope he is.

LYCUS   (Within.)

> Help! Help!

CHORUS

ANTISTROPHE A

> *From the house the song begins* 750
> *I long to hear. That cry*
> *was prelude to his death:*
> *the tyrant's death is near.*

LYCUS   (Within.)

> O land of Cadmus! Treachery! I die!

CHORUS LEADER

> Die: you would have killed. Show your boldness now 755
> as you repay to justice all you owe.

CHORUS

What lying mortal made that fable,
that mindless tale,
that slander on the blessed?
Who denied the gods are strong?

CHORUS LEADER

Old friends, the godless man is dead!   760
The house is silent. Turn to the dances!
Those I love now prosper as I hoped.°

CHORUS

STROPHE B

Let dance and feasting now prevail
throughout this holy town of Thebes!
Joy and mourning change their places,   765
old disaster turns to dancing!
Change now rings my change of song!
The new king's gone to death, the old king rules!
Our king runs home from Hades' harbor!   770
He comes again, he comes, my king and hope,
of whom my hope despaired.

ANTISTROPHE B

The gods of heaven do prevail:
they raise the good and scourge the bad.
Excess of happiness—it drives
men's minds awry; in its train   775
comes on corrupted power.
No man foresees the final stretch of time.
Evil lures him to commit injustice,
until he wrecks at last the somber car
that holds prosperity.   780

STROPHE C

O Ismenus, come with crowns!
Dance and sing: you gleaming streets
of seven-gated Thebes!

Come, O Dirce, lovely fountain.
Leave your father's waters, bring
the nymphs, Asopus' daughters!   785
Come and sing the famous crown
of Heracles the victor!
O wooded crag of Delphi,   790
O Muses' homes on Helicon!
Make my city's walls resound,
echo back the joy of Thebes,
city where the Sown Men rose
with shields of bronze, where still   795
their children's children dwell,
        a blessed light to Thebes!

ANTISTROPHE C

O marriage-bed two bridegrooms shared!
One was man; the other, Zeus,
who entered in the bridal bed   800
and with Alcmene lay.
How true, O Zeus, that marriage
proves to be! Your part therein,
against all doubt, is proven true!
For time at last has clearly shown the strength   805
of Heracles the hero.
You made your way from Pluto's halls;
you left the dungeon underground.
You are to me a better king
than that ignoble lord: 810
comparison made plain
in the struggle of the sword,
if justice still finds favor
        among the blessed gods.

                    (Enter Madness and Iris above the palace.)

CHORUS LEADER
    Ah! Ah!   815

Is the same terror on us all? Look there,
old friends: what phantom hovers on the house?

CHORUS [*singing*]
Fly, fly!
Stir your heavy limbs! Back, away!
Lord Paean, help us! Avert disaster!   820

IRIS
Courage, old men. You see here Madness,
child of Night, and me, servant of the gods,
Iris. We bring no harm upon your city.
Against one man alone our war is waged,   825
him whom men call Alcmene's son by Zeus.
Until his bitter labors had been done,
his fate preserved him; nor would father Zeus
let me or Hera do him any harm.
But now Eurystheus' orders have been done,   830
Hera plans, by making him destroy his sons,
to taint him with fresh murder; and I agree.
          Up, then, unmarried child of blackest Night,
rouse up, harden that relentless heart,
send madness on this man, confound his mind   835
and make him kill his sons. Madden his feet;
drive him, goad him, shake out the sails of death
and make him speed by his own deadly hands
his sons, his own life's glory, to Acheron.
Let him learn what Hera's anger is,   840
and what is mine. For the gods are nothing,
and men prevail, if this one man escape.

MADNESS
I was born of noble birth: my mother
is the Night, and my father is the Sky.
My functions make me loathsome to the gods,°   845
nor do I gladly visit men I love.
And I advise both you and Hera now,

lest I see you stumble, to hear me out.
This man against whose house you drive me on
has won great fame on earth and with the gods.   850
He reclaimed the pathless land and raging sea,
and he alone held up the honors of the gods
when they wilted by the deeds of evil men.
I advise you: renounce these wicked plans.

IRIS

Hera's schemes and mine need no advice from you.   855

MADNESS

I show you the better path: you choose the worse.

IRIS

Hera has not sent you down to show your sanity.

MADNESS

O Sun, you be my witness: I act against my will.
But since I must do this for Hera and follow you,
like a pack of eager hounds together with their huntsman,   860
so go I shall: to the heart of Heracles I run,
more fast, more wild than ocean's groaning breakers,
than earthquake, or the lightning's agonizing bolt!
I shall batter through the roof and leap upon the house!
But first I'll kill his sons. Killing them, he won't know   865
he kills what he begot, until my madness leave him.
        Look: already, head writhing, he leaps the starting post;
jumps and now stops; his eyeballs bulge, and pupils roll;
his breath comes heaving up, a bull about to charge!
And now he bellows up the horrid fates from hell;   870
soon I'll make you dance still more to terror's pipes!
Soar to Olympus, Iris, on your honored way,
while I now sink, unseen, to the house of Heracles.

(Exit Madness down into the palace. Iris flies away.)

CHORUS [*singing in this lyric interchange, with Amphitryon singing in*
reply from within the house]

O city, mourn! Your flower   875
is cut down, the son of Zeus.
O Hellas, mourn! You have lost
your savior! He dances now
to the fatal pipes of madness!

Dreadful, she° has mounted her car;   880
she goads her team!
she drives them hard!
O Gorgon of Night, O Madness,
glittering-eyed, your hundred-snaky head!

Instantly, fortune is reversed by god!   885
Instantly, and father murders sons!

AMPHITRYON
O horror!

CHORUS
O Zeus, your son has lost his sons!
Vengeance, mad, implacable, exacts
the penalty! Disaster lays him low!   890

AMPHITRYON
O my house!

CHORUS
Now the dance begins! Not here,
Bacchus' drums! No lovely thyrsus here!

AMPHITRYON
O my home!

CHORUS
For blood, she drives, for blood!
No wine of Dionysus here!   895

AMPHITRYON

Fly, children, save yourselves!

CHORUS

                             Horrid,

horrid tune of the pipe!
His sons, he hunts them down!
Madness through the house,
madness dancing death!

AMPHITRYON

O grief! 900

CHORUS

I grieve for those two,
for the old man, for the mother
who bore, who nursed her sons in vain!

Look, look!
Whirlwind shakes the house, the roof falls! 905
Ah!

AMPHITRYON°

Ah!
O daughter of Zeus, what are you doing here?
You are sending against this house
ruin that reaches to hell,
as once, Athena, you did against Enceladus!

(Enter Messenger from the palace.)

MESSENGER [*speaking in this interchange with the Chorus, who sing in reply*]

O bodies blanched with age . . . 910

CHORUS

                          Why that cry?

MESSENGER

Horror in the house!

CHORUS

O my prophetic fears!

MESSENGER

The children live no more.

CHORUS

Ah . . .

MESSENGER

Mourn them, grieve them.

CHORUS

Cruel murder,
O cruel hands of a father!   915

MESSENGER

No words could tell the woes that we have suffered.

CHORUS

How did it happen, how this madness,
children killed by a father's hands?
How did disaster strike, madness
hurled from heaven on this house?   920
How did those pitiful children die?

MESSENGER

Offerings to Zeus were set before the hearth
to purify the house, for Heracles
had cast the body of the king outside.
There the children stood, a lovely chorus,   925
with Megara and the old man. In holy hush
the basket made the circle of the altar.
And then, as Heracles reached out his hand
to take the torch and dip it in the water,
he stood stock-still. There he stood, not moving,   930
while the children stared. Suddenly he changed:
his eyes rolled and bulged from their sockets,
and the veins stood out, gorged with blood, and froth

began to trickle down his bearded chin.
Then he spoke, laughing like a maniac: 935
"Why hallow fire, Father, to cleanse the house
before I kill Eurystheus? Why double work,
when at one blow I might complete my task?
I'll go and fetch Eurystheus' head, add it
to those now killed, then purify my hands.   940
Empty your water out! Drop those baskets!
Someone fetch my bow. Someone get my club:
I march against Mycenae! Let me have
crowbars and picks: the Cyclopes built well,
cramping stone on stone with plumb and mallet,   945
but with my pick I'll rip them down again."
Then he fancied that his chariot stood there;
he made as though to leap its rails and ride off,
prodding with his hand as though it held a goad.
        Whether to laugh or shudder, we could not tell.   950
We stared at one another. Then one man asked,
"Is the master playing, or has he gone . . . mad?"
Up and down, throughout the house, he went,
and rushing into the men's hall, claimed it was
Nisus' city. Then going to his chamber°   955
he threw himself to the floor, and acted out
a feast. He walked around a while,° then said
he was approaching Isthmus' wooded valley.
He unstrapped his buckles and stripped himself bare,
and wrestled with no one; then called for silence   960
and crowned himself the victor of a match
that never was. Then he raged against Eurystheus,
and said he was in Mycenae. His father
caught him by that muscled hand and said:
"What do you mean, my son? What is this change   965
in you? Or has the blood of those you've slain
made you mad?" He thought Eurystheus' father
had come, trembling, to supplicate his hand;
pushed him away, and set his bow and arrows

against his sons. He thought he was killing   970
Eurystheus' children. Trembling with terror,
they rushed here and there; one hid beneath
his mother's robes, one ran to the shadow
of a pillar, and the last crouched like a bird
below the altar. Their mother shrieked:
"You are their father! Will you kill your sons?"   975
And shouts broke from the old man and the slaves.
Around the pillar he pursued his son
in dreadful circles, then stopped in front of him
and shot him in the liver. Backward he fell,
dying, and stained the flagstones with his blood.   980
His father shouted in triumph, exulting,
"Here is the first of Eurystheus' fledglings dead;
his death repays me for his father's hate."
He aimed his bow at the second, who crouched
below the altar's base, trying to hide.   985
The boy leaped first, fell at his father's knees
and held his hand up to his father's chin.
"Dearest Father," he cried, "do not murder me.
You're killing your own son, not Eurystheus'!"
But he just stared with stony Gorgon eyes,   990
found his son too close to draw the bow,
and brought his club down on that golden head,
and smashed the skull, just like a blacksmith
smiting steel. Now that his second son lay dead,
he rushed to kill the single victim left.   995
But before he could do this, the mother
seized her child, ran within and locked the doors.
And, as though these were the Cyclopean walls,
he pried the panels up, ripped out the jambs,
and with one arrow brought down son and wife.   1000
And then he rushed to kill his father too,
but look! a vision came—or so it seemed to us—
Pallas, with plumed helm, brandishing a spear.
She hurled a rock; it struck him on the chest,

stopped short his murderous rage and knocked him   1005
into sleep. He slumped to the floor and hit
his back against a pillar which had fallen there,
snapped in two pieces when the roof collapsed.
        Delivered from the fear that made us run,   1010°
we helped the old man lash him down with ropes   1009
against the pillar, lest when he awakes
still greater grief be added to the rest.
He sleeps now, wretched man, no happy sleep,
killer of his wife and sons. I do not know
one man alive more miserable than this.   1015

(Exit Messenger into the palace.)

CHORUS [*singing*]
The hill of Argos had a murder once
Danaus' daughters did, murder's byword,
unbelievable in Hellas!
But murder here has far outrun,
surpassed by far
that dreadful crime.   1020
And Procne's only son was slain,
murdered by his mother's hands and made,
I say, the Muses' sacrifice.°
She had but that one son,
while you, poor wretch, had three,
all murdered by your madness.
What dirge, what song   1025
shall I sing for the dead?
What dance shall I dance for death?

*(The door of the palace opens revealing Heracles asleep, bound to a
broken pillar, surrounded by the bodies of Megara and the children.)*

Ah, look!
Look: the great doors
of the palace open wide!   1030

Look there!
Look: the children's corpses
before their wretched father.
How terribly he lies asleep
after his children's slaughter!

Ropes around his body,   1035
knotted cords bind Heracles,
cables lash him down
to the pillars of his house.

(Enter Amphitryon from the palace.)

CHORUS LEADER [speaking]
  Here the old man comes, moving along
  with heavy steps, mourning in bitterness   1040
  like some bird whose unfledged covey is slain.

AMPHITRYON [singing]
  Hush, old men of Cadmus' city,
  and let him sleep. Hush:
  let him forget his grief.

CHORUS [singing]
  I weep for you, old friend,   1045
  for these boys, and for that head
  that wore the victor's crown.

AMPHITRYON
  Stand further off: not a sound,
  not a cry. His sleep is deep,
  his sleep is calm. Let him lie.

CHORUS
  So much blood . . .   1050

AMPHITRYON
  Hush! you will kill me.

CHORUS
        . . . poured out, piled high!

[55] HERACLES

AMPHITRYON
 Softly, gently, old friends.
 If he awakes and breaks his bonds,   1055
 he will destroy us all:
 father, city, and his house.

CHORUS
 I cannot hold my grief.

AMPHITRYON
                              Hush:
 let me hear his breathing.
 I'll set my ear to him.

CHORUS
 Does he sleep?   1060

AMPHITRYON
                 He sleeps, but sleeps
 as dead men do,° because he slew his wife
 and slew his sons with twanging bow.

CHORUS
 Grieve then, mourn . . .

AMPHITRYON
                     I mourn, I grieve.   1065

CHORUS
 . . . mourn for these dead children . . .

AMPHITRYON
                                    Ah . . .

CHORUS
 . . . and mourn for your son.

AMPHITRYON
                                    Ah . . .

CHORUS
Old friend . . .

AMPHITRYON
            Hush, be still:
he stirs and turns! He wakes! Quick,
let me hide myself inside the house.   1070

CHORUS
Courage: darkness lies upon his eyes.

AMPHITRYON
Take care, take care. My grief is such,
I have no fear to leave the light and die.
But if he murders me who begot him,
he shall add a greater grief to these,   1075
and have on him the curse of father's blood.

CHORUS
Best for you it would have been
if you had died that very day
you took revenge on those who slew
the kinsmen of your wife, the day
you sacked the city of the Taphians!   1080

AMPHITRYON
Run, run, old friends, back from the house,
away! He wakes! Run, run
from his reawakened rage!
Or soon he'll pile murder on murder,
to dance madness through all Thebes!   1085

CHORUS LEADER
O Zeus, why have you hated him so much,
your own son? Why launched him on this sea of grief?

HERACLES   *(Awakening.)*
How now?

I do breathe . . . what I ought to see, I see:
heaven and earth, the gleaming shafts of the sun . . .   1090
But how strangely my muddled senses swim,
as on a choppy sea . . . my breath comes warm,
torn up unsteadily from heaving lungs . . .
And look: I sit here, like a ship lashed tight
with cables binding my chest and arms,   1095
moored to a piece of broken masonry;
and there, close beside me, corpses lie . . .
and my bow and arrows littered on the ground,
those faithful former comrades of my arms,
that guarded my chest, and I guarded them.   1100
Have I come back to Hades? Have I run
Eurystheus' race again? Hades? But how?
No, for I see no rock of Sisyphus,
no Pluto, no Persephone's scepter.
I am bewildered. Where can I be? I'm helpless.   1105
        Help! Is there some friend of mine, near or far,
who will help me in my bewilderment?
For all I took for granted now seems strange . . .

AMPHITRYON [*now speaking*]
    Old friends, shall I approach my affliction?

CHORUS LEADER
    Go, and I'll go with you, sharing in your grief.   1110

HERACLES
    Why do you cry, Father, and veil your eyes?
    Why do you stand off from the son you love?

AMPHITRYON
    O my son, for you're my son, even in misfortune.

HERACLES
    What is my misfortune that you should weep for it?

AMPHITRYON
    Even a god would weep, if he knew it.   1115

[58] EURIPIDES

HERACLES

A great grief it must be; but still you hide it.

AMPHITRYON

It is there to see, if you are sane to see it.

HERACLES

Tell me if you mean my life is not the same.

AMPHITRYON

Tell me if you are sane; then I shall speak.

HERACLES

O gods, how ominous these questions are! 1120

AMPHITRYON

I wonder even now if you are not mad . . .

HERACLES

Mad? I cannot remember being mad.

AMPHITRYON

Friends, shall I loose his ropes? What should I do?

HERACLES

Yes. Tell me who bound me! Who disgraced me so?

AMPHITRYON

This trouble you should know. The rest let go. 1125

HERACLES

I say no more. Will you tell me now?

AMPHITRYON

O Zeus, throned next to Hera, do you see?

HERACLES

Is it from there that my sufferings have come?

AMPHITRYON

Let the goddess go. Shoulder your own grief.

HERACLES

I am ruined. Your words will be disaster.   1130

AMPHITRYON

Look. Look at the bodies of these children.

HERACLES

Oh horrible! What awful sight is this?

AMPHITRYON

Your unnatural war against your sons.

HERACLES

War? What war do you mean? Who killed these boys?

AMPHITRYON

You and your bow and some god are all guilty.   1135

HERACLES

What! I did it? O Father, herald of evil!

AMPHITRYON

You were mad. Your questions ask for grief.

HERACLES

And am I too the murderer of my wife?

AMPHITRYON

All this was the work of your hand alone.

HERACLES

O black night of grief which covers me!   1140

AMPHITRYON

It is because of this you see me weep.

HERACLES

Did I ruin all my house in my madness?

AMPHITRYON

I know but this: everything you have is grief.

HERACLES

Where did my madness take me? Where did I die?

AMPHITRYON

By the altar, as you purified your hands.   1145

HERACLES

Why then am I so sparing of this life,
if I was born to kill my dearest sons?
Let me avenge my children's murder:
let me hurl myself down from some sheer rock,
or drive the whetted sword into my side,   1150
or expunge with fire this body's madness
and burn away this guilt which sticks to my life!

But look: Theseus comes, my friend and kinsman,
intruding on my strategies for death.
And seeing me, the taint of murdered sons   1155
shall enter at the eye of my dearest friend.
What shall I do? Where can this grief be hid?
Oh for wings to fly! To plunge beneath the earth!
Here: let my garments° hide my head in darkness,
in shame, in horror of this deed I did,   1160
and so concealed, I'll shelter him from harm,
and keep pollution from the innocent.

(He covers his head in his clothing.)

(Enter Theseus from the side.)

THESEUS

I come, old man, leading the youth of Athens,
bringing alliance to your son; my men
wait under arms by the stream of Asopus.   1165
A rumor came to Erechtheus' city
that Lycus had seized the scepter of this land
and was engaged in war against your house.
And so, in gratitude to Heracles

who saved me from Hades, I have come,   1170
old man, if you should need a helping hand.
Ah!
What bodies are these scattered on the ground?
Have I arrived too late, preceded here
by some disaster? Who has killed these boys?
That woman lying there, whose wife was she?   1175
Children are not mustered on the field of war:
no, this is some strange new sorrow I find here.

AMPHITRYON [*singing throughout the following interchange with
Theseus, who speaks in response*]
   O lord of the olive-bearing hill . . .

THESEUS
   Why do you address me in these tones of grief?

AMPHITRYON
   . . . see what grief the gods have given.   1180

THESEUS
   Whose children are these over whom you mourn?

AMPHITRYON
   O gods, my son begot these boys,
   begot them, killed them, his own blood.

THESEUS
   Unsay those words!°

AMPHITRYON
                              Would that I could!   1185

THESEUS
   Oh horrible tale!

AMPHITRYON
                         We are ruined and lost.

THESEUS
   How did it happen? Tell me how.

AMPHITRYON

Dead in the blow of madness,
by arrows dipped in the blood
of the hundred-headed Hydra . . .   1190

THESEUS

This is Hera's war. Who lies there by the bodies?

AMPHITRYON

My son, my most unhappy son,
who fought with giant-killing spear
beside the gods at Phlegraea.

THESEUS

What mortal man was ever cursed like this?   1195

AMPHITRYON

Among all men you would not find
greater toils, greater suffering
                     than this.

THESEUS

Why does he hide his head beneath his robes?

AMPHITRYON

Shame of meeting your eye,
shame before a friend and kinsman,   1200
shame for his murdered sons.

THESEUS

I come to share his grief. Uncover him.

AMPHITRYON   (To Heracles.)

My son, drop your robe from your eyes,
show your forehead to the sun.   1205
An equal weight of supplication comes
to counterpoise your grief.
O my son, I implore you,
by your beard, your knees, your hand,
by an old man's tears: 1210

tame that lion of your rage
that roars you on to death,
yoking grief to grief.

THESEUS   (*To Heracles.*)
   I call on you, huddled there in misery:
   lift up your head and show your face to friends.   1215
   There is no cloud whose utter blackness
   could conceal in night a sorrow like yours.
   Why wave me off, warning me of dread?
   Are you afraid mere words would pollute me?
   What do I care if your misfortunes fall   1220
   on me? You were my good fortune once:
   you saved me from the dead, brought me back to light.
   I loathe a friend whose gratitude grows old,
   a friend who shares his friend's prosperity
   but will not voyage with him in his grief.   1225
   Rise up; uncover that afflicted head
   and look on us. This is courage in a man:
   to bear unflinchingly what heaven° sends.

(*Heracles uncovers his head.*)

HERACLES
   Theseus, have you seen this field of fallen sons?

THESEUS
   I'd heard. I see the grief to which you point.   1230

HERACLES
   How could you then uncloak me to the sun?

THESEUS
   No mortal man can stain what is divine.

HERACLES
   Away, rash friend! Flee my foul pollution.

THESEUS
   Where there is love, no vengeful spirit comes.

HERACLES

I thank you. I helped you once: I don't refuse.   1235

THESEUS

You saved me then, and now I pity you.

HERACLES

A man to be pitied? I slew my children!

THESEUS

I mourn the woes of others for your sake.

HERACLES

Have you ever seen more misery than this?

THESEUS

Your wretchedness towers up and reaches heaven.   1240

HERACLES

And for that reason I'm prepared to die.°

THESEUS

What do you think the gods care for your threats?

HERACLES

Heaven is proud. And I am proud toward heaven.

THESEUS

No more: your presumption will be punished.

HERACLES

My hold is full: there is no room for more.   1245

THESEUS

What will you do? Where does your anger run?

HERACLES

To death: to go back whence I came, beneath the earth.

THESEUS

These are the words of an ordinary man.

HERACLES

Will you, who did not suffer, preach to me?

THESEUS

Is this that Heracles who endured so much? 1250

HERACLES

Not this much. Even endurance has an end.

THESEUS

Mankind's benefactor, man's greatest friend?

HERACLES

What good are men to me? Hera rules.

THESEUS

You die so foolishly? Hellas forbids it.

HERACLES

Listen: let me tell you what makes a mock 1255
at your advice. Let me show you my life:
a life not worth living now, or ever.
Take my father first, a man who killed
my mother's father and, having such a curse,
married Alcmene who gave birth to me. 1260
When a house is built on poor foundations,
then its descendants are the heirs of grief.
Then Zeus—whoever Zeus may be—begot me
for Hera's hatred. Take no offense, old man,
for I count you my father now, not Zeus. 1265
While I was still at suck, she set her snakes
with Gorgon eyes to slither in my crib
and strangle me. And when I grew older
and a belt of muscle bound my body—
why recite all those labors I endured? 1270
All those wars I fought, those beasts I slew,
those lions and triple-bodied Typhons,
Giants, and four-legged Centaur hordes!
I killed the Hydra, that brute whose heads
grew back as soon as lopped. My countless labors done, 1275

I descended down among the sullen dead
to do Eurystheus' bidding and bring to light
the triple-headed hound who guards the gates of hell.
        And now my last worst labor has been done:
I slew my children and crowned my house with grief.   1280
And this is how it is: I cannot stay
at Thebes, the town I love. If I remain,
what temple, what assembly of my friends
will have me? My curse is unapproachable.
Go to Argos then? No, I am banished there.   1285
Settle in some other city then,
where notoriety shall pick me out
to be watched and goaded by bitter gibes°—
"Is this the son of Zeus, who killed his wife
and sons? Away with him! Let him die elsewhere."   1290
To a man who prospers and is blessed,°
all change is grief; but the man who lives
akin to trouble minds disaster less.
But to this pitch of grief my life will come:
the earth itself will groan, forbidding me   1295
to touch the ground, rivers and seas cry out
against my crossing over, and I'll be
like Ixion, bound forever to a wheel.
This is the best, that I be seen no more°
in Hellas, where I prospered and was great.   1300
Why should I live? What profit have I,
having a life both useless and accursed?
Let the noble wife of Zeus begin the dance,
pounding with her feet Olympus' gleaming floors!
For she accomplished what her heart desired,   1305
and hurled the greatest man of Hellas down
in utter ruin. Who would offer prayers
to such a goddess? Jealous of Zeus
for a mortal woman's sake, she has destroyed
Hellas' greatest friend, though he was guiltless.   1310

CHORUS LEADER°
No other god is implicated here,
except the wife of Zeus. Rightly you judge.

THESEUS
My advice is this, rather than suffer ill.°
Fate exempts no man; all humans suffer,
and so the gods too, unless the poets lie.   1315
Do not the gods commit adultery?
Have they not cast their fathers into chains,
in pursuit of power? Yet all the same,
despite their crimes, they live upon Olympus.
How dare you then, mortal that you are,   1320
to protest your fate, when the gods do not?
          Obey the law and leave your native Thebes
and follow after me to Pallas' city.
There I shall purify your hands of blood,
give you a home and a share of my wealth.   1325
All those gifts I have because I killed
the Minotaur and saved twice seven youths,
I cede to you. Everywhere throughout my land,
plots of earth have been reserved for me.
These I now assign to you, to bear your name   1330
until you die. And when you go to Hades,
Athens shall raise you up great monuments
of stone, and honor you with sacrifice.°
And so my city, helping a noble man,
shall win from Hellas a lovely crown of fame.   1335
This thanks and this return I make you now,
who saved me once. For now you need a friend.
He needs no friends who has the love of gods.°
For when god helps a man, he has help enough.

HERACLES
Ah, all this has no bearing on my grief;   1340
but I do not believe the gods commit

adultery, or bind each other in chains.
I never did believe it; I never shall;
nor that one god is tyrant of the rest.
If god is truly god, he is perfect,   1345
lacking nothing. Those are poets' wretched lies.
        Even in my misery I asked myself,
would it not be cowardice to die?
The man who cannot bear up under fate
could never face the weapons of a man.   1350
I shall prevail against death. I shall go
to your city. I accept with thanks your countless gifts.
For countless were the labors I endured;
never yet have I refused, never yet
have I wept, and never did I think   1355
that I should come to this: tears in my eyes.
But now, I see, I must serve necessity.

                                        (To Amphitryon.)

        So, now you see me banished, old man;
you see in me the killer of my sons.
Give them to the grave, give them the tribute   1360
of your tears, for the law forbids me this.
Let them lie there in their mother's arms,
united in their grief, as they were then,
before, in wretched ignorance, I killed her.
And when the earth has hidden their remains,
live on in this city here, even though it hurts.   1365
Compel your soul to bear misfortune with me.°
        O my sons, the father who gave you life
has slain you all, and never shall you reap
that harvest of my life, all I labored for,
that heritage of fame I toiled to leave you.   1370
You too, poor wife, I killed: unkind return
for having kept the honor of my bed,
for all your weary vigil in my house.

O wretched wife and sons! And wretched me!
In grief I now unyoke myself from you.   1375
O bitter sweetness of this last embrace!

O my weapons, bitter partners of my life!
What shall I do? Let you go, or keep you,
knocking against my ribs and always saying,
"With us you murdered wife and sons. Wearing us,   1380
you wear your children's killers." Can I still carry them?
What can I reply? Yet, naked of these weapons,
with which I did the greatest deeds in Hellas,
must I die in shame at my enemies' hands?
No, they must be kept; but in pain I keep them.   1385
        Hold with me, Theseus, in one thing more.
Help me take to Argos the monstrous dog,
lest, alone and desolate of sons, I die.
        O land of Cadmus, O people of Thebes,
mourn with me, grieve with me, attend my children   1390
to the grave! And with one voice mourn us all,
the dead and me. For all of us have died,
all struck down by one blow of Hera's hate.

THESEUS
Rise up, unfortunate friend. Have done with tears.

HERACLES
I cannot rise. My limbs are rooted here.   1395

THESEUS
Yes, necessity breaks even the strong.

HERACLES
Oh to be a stone! To feel no grief!

THESEUS
Enough. Give your hand to your helping friend.

HERACLES
Take care. I may pollute your clothes with blood.

THESEUS

Pollute them then. Spare not. I do not care.   1400

HERACLES

My sons are dead; now you shall be my son.

THESEUS

Place your arm round my neck and I shall lead you.

HERACLES

A yoke of love, but one of us in grief.
O Father, choose a man like this for friend.

AMPHITRYON

The land that gave him birth has noble sons.   1405

HERACLES

Theseus, turn me back. Let me see my sons.

THESEUS

Is this a remedy to ease your grief?

HERACLES

I long for it, and yearn to embrace my father.

AMPHITRYON

My arms embrace you. I want what you want.

THESEUS

Have you forgotten your labors so far?   1410

HERACLES

All those labors I endured were less than these.

THESEUS

If someone sees your weakness, he will not praise you.

HERACLES

Am I so low? You did not think so once.

THESEUS

Once, no. But now where is famous Heracles?

HERACLES
What were you when you were underground?   1415

THESEUS
In courage I was the least of men.

HERACLES
Then will you say my grief degrades me now?

THESEUS
Forward!

HERACLES
                    Farewell, father!

AMPHITRYON
                                        Farewell, my son.

HERACLES
Bury my children.

AMPHITRYON
                            Who will bury me?

HERACLES
                                                    I.

AMPHITRYON
When will you come?

HERACLES
                                        After you die, dear father.°   1420

AMPHITRYON
How?

HERACLES
            I shall have you brought from Thebes to Athens.°
Convey my children in, a grim conveyance,
while I, who have destroyed my house in shame,
am towed in Theseus' wake like some cargo boat.

The man who would prefer great wealth or strength   1425
more than love, more than friends, is diseased of soul.

CHORUS [*chanting*]
We go in grief, we go in tears,
who lose in you our greatest friend.

(*Theseus and Heracles leave to one side, the Chorus to the other.*
Exit Amphitryon into the palace; the door closes behind him,
concealing the bodies of Megara and the children.)

THE TROJAN
WOMEN

Translated by RICHMOND LATTIMORE

THE TROJAN WOMEN: INTRODUCTION

The Play: Date and Composition

External evidence indicates that *The Trojan Women* was most likely produced in 415 BCE, as the third play of a tetralogy with *Alexander*, *Palamedes*, and the satyr-play *Sisyphus* (all lost). Unusually for Euripides, all three tragedies were thus drawn from the same body of mythic material involving the Trojan War: *Alexander* (of which quite substantial fragments survive) dealt with the rediscovery of Paris as an adult after he had been exposed as an infant, *Palamedes* with Odysseus' treachery by which he tricked the Greeks into killing their fellow soldier Palamedes. Though the three plays did not form a single coherently connected narrative of the sort Aeschylus seems to have favored in his trilogies, they did present the three episodes in chronological order and were linked with one another by various shared themes. In the competition that year, Euripides came in second to the obscure playwright Xenocles' tetralogy of *Oedipus*, *Lycaon*, *The Bacchae*, and the satyr-play *Athamas* (all lost).

A few months before the date on which, according to most scholars, the play was produced, the Athenians had captured the small Greek island of Melos and slaughtered all the adult men and enslaved all the women and children. Under the circumstances, it is difficult not to see Euripides' play, with its extended reflection on the piteous fate of a defeated city and its people, as being colored by that recent event.

The Myth

Euripides' *Trojan Women* portrays the fall of Troy from the point of view of the defeated: given that all the Trojan men have been slain by the Greek victors, it is their women—mothers, daughters, wives—who give voice to the suffering of the city. The play begins with the two gods Poseidon and Athena setting aside their previous opposition during the Trojan War and amicably negotiating the destruction of the victorious Greeks for their sacrilege during the sack of the city. But then it moves to a purely human level of unrelieved distress focused above all on Hecuba, the aged former queen of the city, and her family. In contrast to the play *Hecuba*, here the woman who had ruled Troy and, with her, all the defeated Trojan women and children are deprived not only of the act of vengeance, but even of the bare hope for it. Amid the laments of the chorus of anonymous Trojan captives, the various members of Hecuba's family are assigned as slaves or concubines to their future Greek masters; the prophetess Cassandra exults over the death of Agamemnon, which she can foresee; Hector's widow Andromache announces that Polyxena has been sacrificed to the dead Achilles (in contrast to *Hecuba*, Polyxena's death is much less prominent here); and Andromache's young son Astyanax is carried off to be hurled down from the city's walls. Then Helen, Menelaus' wife, whose elopement with the Trojan prince Paris (a son of Hecuba and Priam) had caused the war, debates with Menelaus and Hecuba about how much she should be blamed for what has happened and whether or not she ought to be punished; Menelaus promises to have her killed when they arrive home in Sparta (but we know he will not do so). Finally the corpse of little Astyanax is brought on stage and mourned, and Hecuba and the remaining Trojan women leave to sail off with Odysseus, to whom she has been assigned.

The bloody and heart-rending aftermath of the Trojan War— including all the episodes dramatized here—was extensively depicted in ancient Greek epic, lyric poetry, and art. Euripides himself chose to base a number of different tragedies upon these stories. For example, about ten years before he wrote *The Trojan Women*, he had dramatized later events in *Andromache*. In *Hecuba*, written about nine years before *The Trojan Women*, he portrayed many of the same incidents as he does here. So the main events of this play are likely to have been well known to Euripides' audience already, though the formal and rather legalistic debate between Helen and Hecuba seems characteristically Euripidean and in this form is probably his invention. The play seeks to create an effect upon its audience less by surprise and original plot inventions than by its exploration of the traumatic consequences of war and its almost unrelieved, yet lyrical, portrayal of loss and displacement.

Transmission and Reception

The Trojan Women was not especially popular in antiquity, certainly much less so than *Hecuba*, which treats much of the same legendary material. For example, only a couple of papyri of the play have survived, containing fragments of a plot summary and of some lines. But it did end up being selected as one of the ten canonical plays most studied and read in antiquity. As a result, it is transmitted by three medieval manuscripts and is equipped with ancient and medieval commentaries.

Greek and Latin authors who portrayed Hecuba's sufferings after the fall of Troy inevitably drew upon this play and upon *Hecuba*. Roman tragedies by Ennius (*Andromache*) and Accius (*Astyanax*) are lost; but Seneca's *Troades* (*Trojan Women*) does survive, containing many close echoes of this play of Euripides along with others from his *Hecuba*, and was widely read during the Renaissance. Epic poets like Virgil, Ovid, and Quintus of Smyrna also followed the outlines of Euripides' plot at least in part and presumed their readers' familiarity with his text; and Hecuba eventually became a standard example for the vicissitudes of fortune.

Although during the Middle Ages and Renaissance *The Trojan Women* was largely overshadowed by *Hecuba* (and Seneca), things have been very different in modern times. Already in the middle of the nineteenth century, Hector Berlioz based the first two acts of his opera *Les Troyennes* (1856-59) not only, unsurprisingly, upon Virgil's *Aeneid* but also, innovatively, upon *The Trojan Women*. Since the mid-twentieth century, the experience of the horrors of war, along with changes in dramatic taste, have led to a remarkable resurgence in the play's popularity, and in recent decades it has been one of the most frequently staged of all Greek tragedies. The play has been successfully adapted by such authors as Jean-Paul Sartre (*The Trojan Women*, 1965), Suzuki Tadashi (1974), Hanoch Levin (*The Lost Women of Troy*, 1984), Andrei Serban (1974/1996; with music by Elizabeth Swados), Charles Mee (n.d.), and Ellen McLaughlin (2008). It has also been the subject of notable films by such directors as the Mexican Sergio Véjar (*Las Troyanas*, 1963) and the Greek Michael Cacoyannis (*The Trojan Women*, 1971, starring Katharine Hepburn, Vanessa Redgrave, and Irene Papas).

THE TROJAN WOMEN

Characters   POSEIDON
                ATHENA
                HECUBA, former queen of Troy
                TALTHYBIUS, herald of the Greeks
                CASSANDRA, daughter of Priam and Hecuba
                ANDROMACHE, widow of Hector
                ASTYANAX, young son of Hector and
                Andromache (silent character)
                MENELAUS, co-leader of the Greek army
                HELEN, wife of Menelaus
                CHORUS of Trojan women

*Scene: An open space before the walls of the ruined city of Troy, with
a tent that temporarily houses the captive women. As the play opens,
Hecuba is lying on the ground in front of the tent.*

                      (Enter Poseidon above the scene.)

POSEIDON
   I am Poseidon. I come from the Aegean depths
   of the sea beneath whose waters Nereid choirs evolve
   the intricate bright circle of their dancing feet.
   For since that day when Phoebus Apollo and I laid down
   on Trojan soil the close of these stone walls, drawn true   5
   and straight, there has always been affection in my heart
   unfading for these Phrygians and for their city,
   which smolders now, fallen before the Argive spears,

ruined, sacked, gutted. Such is Athena's work, and his,
the Parnassian, Epeius of Phocis, architect   10
and builder of the horse that swarmed with inward steel,
that fatal bulk which passed within the battlements,
whose fame hereafter shall be loud among men unborn,°
the wooden horse, which hid the secret spears within.
Now the gods' groves are desolate, their thrones of power   15
blood-spattered where beside the lift of the altar steps
of Zeus Defender, Priam was cut down and died.
The ships of the Achaeans load with spoils of Troy
now, the piled gold of Phrygia. And the men of Greece
who made this expedition and took the city stay   20
only for the favoring stern-wind now to greet their wives
and children after ten years' harvests wasted here.

The will of Argive Hera and Athena won
its way against my will. Between them they broke Troy.
So I must leave my altars and great Ilium,   25
since once a city sinks into sad desolation
the gods' state sickens also, and their worship fades.
Scamander's valley echoes to the wail of slaves,
the captive women given to their masters now,
some to Arcadia or the men of Thessaly   30
assigned, or to the lords of Athens, Theseus' strain;
while all the women of Troy yet unassigned are here
beneath the shelter of these walls, chosen to wait
the will of princes, and among them Tyndareus' child
Helen of Sparta, treated—rightly—as a captive slave.   35

Nearby, beside the gates, for any to look upon
who has the heart, she lies face upward, Hecuba,
weeping for multitudes her multitude of tears.
Polyxena, one daughter, even now was killed
in secrecy and pain beside Achilles' tomb.   40
Priam is gone, their children dead; one girl is left,
the maiden Cassandra, crazed by Lord Apollo's stroke,

whom Agamemnon, in despite of the gods' will
and all religion, will lead by force to his secret bed.

O city, long ago a happy place, good-bye;   45
good-bye, hewn bastions. Pallas, child of Zeus, did this.
But for her hatred, you might stand strong-founded still.

(Enter Athena above the scene.)

ATHENA

August among the gods, O vast divinity,
closest in kinship to Zeus the father of all, may one
who quarreled with you in the past make peace, and speak?   50

POSEIDON

You may, lady Athena; for the strands of kinship,
close drawn, work no small magic to enchant the mind.

ATHENA

I thank you for your gentleness, and bring you now
questions whose issue touches you and me, my lord.

POSEIDON

Is this the annunciation of some new word spoken   55
by Zeus, or any other of the divinities?

ATHENA

No; but for Troy's sake, on whose ground we stand, I come
to win the favor of your power, as my ally.

POSEIDON

You hated Troy once; did you throw your hate away
and change to pity, now its walls are black with fire?   60

ATHENA

Come back to the question. Will you take counsel with me
and help me gladly in all that I would bring to pass?

POSEIDON

I will indeed; but tell me what you wish to do.
Are you here for the Achaeans' or the Phrygians' sake?

ATHENA

For the Trojans, whom I hated this short time since,   65
to make the Achaeans' homecoming a thing of sorrow.

POSEIDON

This is a springing change of character. Why must
you hate too hard, and love too hard, your loves and hates?

ATHENA

Did you not know they outraged my temple, and shamed me?

POSEIDON

I know that Ajax dragged Cassandra thence by force.   70

ATHENA

And the Achaeans did nothing. They did not even speak.

POSEIDON

Yet they captured Ilium by your strength alone.

ATHENA

True; therefore help me. I would do some evil to them.

POSEIDON

I am ready for anything you ask. What will you do?

ATHENA

Make their home voyage a most unhappy coming home.   75

POSEIDON

While they stay here ashore, or out on the deep sea?

ATHENA

When they take ship from Ilium and set sail for home
Zeus will shower down his rainstorms and the weariless beat
of hail, to make black the bright air with roaring winds.
He has promised my hand the gift of the blazing thunderbolt   80
to dash and overwhelm with fire the Achaean ships.
Yours is your own domain, the Aegean crossing. Make
the sea thunder to the tripled wave and spinning surf,
cram thick the hollow Euboean fold with floating dead;

so after this Greeks may learn how to use with fear   85
my sacred places, and respect all gods beside.

POSEIDON

This shall be done, and joyfully. It needs no long
discourse to tell you. I will shake the Aegean Sea.
Myconos' headlands and the swine-back reefs of Delos,
the Capherean promontories, Scyros, Lemnos   90
shall take the washed-up bodies of men drowned at sea.
Back to Olympus now; gather the thunderbolts
from your father's hands, then take your watcher's post, to wait
the chance, when the Achaean fleet puts out to sea.
That mortal who sacks fallen cities is a fool   95
if he gives the temples and the tombs, the hallowed places
of the dead, to desolation. His own turn must come.

(Exit Poseidon and Athena. Hecuba rises slowly to her feet.)

HECUBA [chanting]

Rise, stricken head, from the dust;
lift up the throat. This is Troy, but Troy
and we, Troy's kings, are perished.   100
Stoop to the changing fortune.
Steer for the crossing and your fortune,
hold not life's prow on the course against
wave beat and accident.
Ah me,   105
what need I further for tears' occasion,
state perished, my sons, and my husband?
O massive pride that my fathers heaped
to magnificence, you meant nothing.
Must I be hushed? Were it better thus?   110
Should I cry a lament?
Unhappy, accursed,
limbs cramped, I lie
backed on this stiff bed.
O head, O temples   115

and sides; sweet, to shift,
let the tired spine rest,
weight eased by the sides alternate,
against the strain of the tears' song
where stricken people find music yet   120
in the song undanced of their wretchedness.

[singing]
You ships' prows, that the rapid
oars swept here to blessed Ilium
over the sea's blue water
and the placid harbors of Hellas   125
to the pipes' grim beat
and the swing of the shrill boat whistles;
you made the crossing, made fast ashore
the Egyptians' skill, the sea cables,
alas, by the coasts of Troy;   130
it was you, ships, that carried the fatal bride
of Menelaus, her brother Castor's shame,
the stain on the Eurotas.
Now she has killed
the sire of the fifty sons,   135
Priam; me, unhappy Hecuba,
she drove on this reef of ruin.
Such state I keep
to sit by the tents of Agamemnon.
I am led captive   140
from my house, an old, unhappy woman,
like my city ruined and pitiful.
Come then, sad wives of the Trojans
whose spears were bronze,
their daughters, brides of disaster,
let us mourn the smoke of Ilium.   145
And I, as among winged birds
the mother, lead out
the clashing cry, the song; not that song

wherein once long ago,
when Priam leaned on his scepter,   150
my feet were queens of the choir and led
the proud dance to the gods of Phrygia.

(Enter the First Half-Chorus from the tent.)

FIRST HALF-CHORUS [singing this lyric interchange with Hecuba,
who continues to sing in reply]

STROPHE A

Hecuba, what are these cries?
What news now? Through the tent walls
I heard your pitiful weeping,   155
and fear shivered in the breasts
of the Trojan women, who within
sob out the day of their slavery.

HECUBA

My children, the ships of the Argives
will move today. The hand is at the oar.   160

FIRST HALF-CHORUS

They will? Why? Must I take ship
so soon from the land of my fathers?

HECUBA

I know nothing. I look for disaster.

FIRST HALF-CHORUS

Alas!
Poor women of Troy, torn from your homes,   165
come, hear of miseries.
The Argives push for home.

HECUBA

Oh,
let her not come forth,
not now, my child
Cassandra, driven delirious   170
to shame us before the Argives,
not the mad one, to bring fresh pain to my pain.

Ah no.
Troy, ill-starred Troy, this is the end;
your last sad people leave you now, 175
both living and broken.

(Enter the Second Half-Chorus from the tent.)

SECOND HALF-CHORUS [*singing, while Hecuba continues to sing
in reply*]
ANTISTROPHE A
Ah me. Trembling, I left the tents
of Agamemnon to listen.
Tell us, our queen. Did the Argive council
decree my death?
Or are the seamen manning the ships now, 180
oars ready for action?

HECUBA
My child, I have come stunned with terror in my soul,
awake ever since the dawn.

SECOND HALF-CHORUS
Has a herald come from the Danaans yet?
Whose wretched slave shall I be ordained? 185

HECUBA
You are near the lots now.

SECOND HALF-CHORUS
Alas!
Who will lead me away? An Argive?
To an island home? To Phthiotis?
Unhappy, surely, and far from Troy.

HECUBA
And I, 190
whose wretched slave
shall I be? Where, in my gray age,
a faint drone,
poor image of a corpse,

weak shining among dead men? Shall
I stand and keep guard at their doors,
shall I nurse their children, I who in Troy   195
held state as a princess?

(The two Half-Choruses now unite to form a single Chorus.)

CHORUS [all singing together]
STROPHE B

So pitiful, so pitiful
your shame and your lamentation.
No longer shall I move the shifting pace
of the shuttle at the looms of Ida.   200
I shall look no more on the houses of my parents.°
No more. I shall have worse troubles.
Shall I be forced to the bed of Greek masters?
I curse that night and my fortune.
Must I draw the water of Peirene,   205
a servant at sacred springs?
Might I only be taken to Athens, domain
of Theseus, the bright, the blessed!
Never to the whirl of Eurotas, not Sparta   210
detested, who gave us Helen,
not look with slave's eyes on the scourge
of Troy, Menelaus.

ANTISTROPHE B

I have heard the rumor
of the hallowed ground by Peneus,   215
bright doorstone of Olympus,
deep burdened in beauty of wealth and harvest.
There would I be next after the blessed,
the sacrosanct land of Theseus.
And they say that the land of Aetna,   220
the keep against Punic men,
mother of Sicilian mountains, sounds
in the herald's cry for games' garlands;

and the land washed
by the streaming Ionian Sea,   225
that land watered by the loveliest
of rivers, Crathis, that turns hair red-gold
and draws from the depths of sacred wells
blessings on a strong people.
[*chanting*]
See now, from the host of the Danaans   230
the herald, charged with new orders, takes
the speed of his way toward us.
What message? What command? Since we count as slaves
even now in the Dorian kingdom.

(*Talthybius enters from the side, accompanied by some soldiers.*)

TALTHYBIUS

Hecuba, incessantly my ways have led me to Troy   235
as the messenger of all the Achaean armament.
You know me from the old days, my lady; I am sent,
Talthybius, with new messages for you to hear.

HECUBA [*singing in this interchange with Talthybius, who speaks
in reply*]

It comes, beloved daughters of Troy; the thing I feared.

TALTHYBIUS

You are all given your masters now. Was this your dread?   240

HECUBA

Ah, yes. Is it Phthia, then? A city of Thessaly?
Tell me. The land of Cadmus?

TALTHYBIUS

All are allotted separately, each to a man.

HECUBA

Who is given to whom? Oh, is there any hope
left for the women of Troy?   245

TALTHYBIUS

I understand. Yet ask not for all, but for each apart.

HECUBA

Who was given my child? Tell me, who shall be lord
of my poor abused Cassandra?

TALTHYBIUS

King Agamemnon chose her. She was given to him.

HECUBA

Slave woman to that Lacedaemonian wife?
My unhappy child!   250

TALTHYBIUS

No. Rather to be joined with him in a dark bed of love.

HECUBA

She, Apollo's virgin, blessed in the privilege
the gold-haired god gave her, a life forever unwed?

TALTHYBIUS

Love's archery and the prophetic maiden struck him hard.   255

HECUBA

Dash down, my daughter,
the twigs of your consecration,
break the god's garlands to your throat gathered.

TALTHYBIUS

Is it not high favor to be brought to a king's bed?

HECUBA

And my poor youngest whom you took away,
where is she?°   260

TALTHYBIUS

You spoke now of Polyxena. Is it not so?

HECUBA

To whose arms did the lot force her?

TALTHYBIUS

She is given a guardianship, to serve Achilles' tomb.

HECUBA

To serve, my child? Over a tomb?   265
Tell me, is this their way,
some law, friend, established among the Greeks?

TALTHYBIUS

Speak of your child in words of blessing. She feels no pain.

HECUBA

What did that mean? Does she live in the sunlight still?

TALTHYBIUS

She lives her destiny, and her cares are over now.   270

HECUBA

And the wife of bronze-embattled Hector: tell me of her,
Andromache the forlorn. What shall she suffer now?

TALTHYBIUS

The son of Achilles chose her. She was given to him.

HECUBA

And I, my aged frailty crutched for support on staves,   275
whom shall I serve?

TALTHYBIUS

You shall be slave to Odysseus, lord of Ithaca.

HECUBA

Oh no, no!
Tear the shorn head,
rip nails through both cheeks.   280
Must I?
To be given as slave to serve that vile, that slippery man,
right's enemy, brute, murderous beast,
that mouth of lies and treachery, that makes void   285
faith in things promised

and turns to hate what was beloved! Oh, mourn,
daughters of Ilium, weep as one for me.
I am gone, doomed, undone,
O wretched, given 290
the worst lot of all.

CHORUS LEADER

You know your destiny now, Queen Hecuba. But mine?
What Hellene, what Achaean is my master now?

TALTHYBIUS

Men-at-arms, do your duty. Bring Cassandra forth
without delay. Our orders are to deliver her 295
to the general at once. And afterward we can bring
to the rest of the princes their allotted captive women.
But see! What is that burst of a torch flame inside?
What can it mean? Are the Trojan women setting fire
to their chambers, at point of being torn from their land 300
to sail for Argos? Have they set themselves aflame
in longing for death? I know it is the way of freedom
in times like these to stiffen the neck against disaster.
Open, there, open; let not the fate desired by these,
dreaded by the Achaeans, hurl their wrath on me. 305

(Enter Cassandra from the tent, carrying a flaming torch.)

HECUBA [*now speaking*]

You are wrong, they're not setting fires. It is my Cassandra
whirled out on running feet in the passion of her frenzy.

CASSANDRA [*singing*]

STROPHE

Lift up, heave up; carry the flame; I bring fire of worship,
torches to the temple.
Io, Hymen, my lord! Hymenaeus! 310
Blessed the bridegroom.
Blessed am I indeed to lie at a king's side,
blessed the bride of Argos.

Hymen, my lord, Hymenaeus!
Yours were the tears, my mother, 315
yours was the lamentation for my father fallen,
for your city so dear beloved,
but mine this marriage, my marriage,
and I shake out the torch flare, 320
brightness, dazzle,
light for you, Hymenaeus,
Hecate, light for you,
for the bed of virginity as man's custom ordains.

ANTISTROPHE

Let your feet dance, rippling the air; let the chorus go, 325
as when my father's fate went in blessedness.
O sacred circle of dance.
Lead now, Phoebus Apollo; I wear your laurel,
I tend your temple, 330
Hymen, O Hymenaeus!
Dance, Mother, dance, laugh; lead; let your feet
wind in the shifting pattern and follow mine,
keep the sweet step with me,
cry out the name Hymenaeus 335
and the bride's name in the shrill
and the blessed incantation.
O you daughters of Phrygia robed in splendor,
dance for my wedding,
for the husband fate appointed to lie beside me. 340

CHORUS LEADER

Can you not, Queen Hecuba, stop this bacchanal before
her light feet whirl her away into the Argive camp?

HECUBA

Fire God, in mortal marriages you lift up your torch,
but here you throw a melancholy light, not seen
through my hopes that went so high in days gone past.
    O child, 345

there never was a time I dreamed you'd wed like this,
like this, at spear's edge, under force of Argive arms.
Let me take the light; crazed, passionate, you cannot carry
it straight enough, poor child. Your fate is intemperate
as you are, always. There is no relief for you.   350

(Hecuba takes the torch from Cassandra and
gives it to some Trojan women.)

You Trojan women, take the torch inside, and change
to songs of tears this poor girl's marriage melodies.

(Exit these women with the torch into the tent.)

CASSANDRA
O Mother, star my hair with flowers of victory.
This is a king I marry; then be glad; escort   355
the bride—and if she falters, thrust her strongly on.
If Loxias lives, the Achaeans' pride, great Agamemnon
has won a wife more fatal than ever Helen was.
Since I will kill him, and avenge my brothers' blood
and my father's in the desolation of his house.   360
But I leave this in silence and sing not now the axe
to drop against my throat and other throats than mine,
the agony of the mother murdered, brought to pass
from our marriage rites, and Atreus' house made desolate.
I am ridden by god's curse still, yet I will step so far   365
out of my frenzy as to show our city's fate
is blessed beyond the Achaeans'. For one woman's sake,
one act of love, these hunted Helen down and threw
thousands of lives away. Their general—clever man—
in the name of a vile woman cut his darling down,   370
gave up for a brother the sweetness of children in his house,
all to bring back that brother's wife, a woman who went
of her free will, not caught in constraint of violence.
The Achaeans came beside Scamander's banks, and died
day after day, though none sought to wrench their land from
    them   375

nor their own towering cities. Those the war god caught
never saw their sons again, nor were they laid to rest
decently in winding sheets by their wives' hands, but lie
buried in alien ground; while all went wrong at home
as the widows perished, and couples who had raised in vain   380
their children were left childless, no one left to tend
their tombs and give to them the sacrificial blood.
For such success as this congratulate the Greeks.°
No, but the shame is better left in silence, for fear
my singing voice become the voice of wretchedness.   385
The Trojans have that glory which is loveliest:
they died for their own country. So the bodies of all
who took the spears were carried home in loving hands,
brought, in the land of their fathers, to the embrace of earth
and buried becomingly as the rite fell due. The rest,   390
those Phrygians who escaped death in battle, day by day
came home to happiness the Achaeans could not know;
their wives, their children. Then was Hector's fate so sad?
You think so. Listen to the truth. He is dead and gone
surely, but with reputation, as a valiant man.   395
How could this be, except for the Achaeans' coming?
Had they held back, none might have known how great he
    was.
The bride of Paris was the daughter of Zeus. Had he
not married her, his wife's name would sleep in endless
    silence.
Though surely the wise man will forever shrink from war,   400
yet if war come, the hero's death will lay a wreath
not lusterless on the city. The coward alone brings shame.
Let no more tears fall, Mother, for our land, nor for
this marriage I make; it is by marriage that I bring
to destruction those whom you and I have hated most.   405

CHORUS LEADER
    You smile on your disasters. Can it be that you
    some day will invalidate the darkness of this song?

TALTHYBIUS

Were it not that Apollo has driven wild your wits
I would make you sorry for sending the princes of our host
on their way home in augury of foul speech like this.   410
Now pride of majesty and wisdom's outward show
have fallen to stature less than what was nothing worth
since he, almighty prince of the assembled Hellenes,
Atreus' son beloved, has stooped—by his own will—
to find his love in a crazed girl. I, a plain man,   415
would not marry this woman or keep her as my lover.
You then, with your wits unhinged by idiocy,
your scolding of Argos and your Trojans glorified
I throw to the winds to scatter them. Come now with me
to the ships, a bride—and such a bride—for Agamemnon.   420

Hecuba, when Laertes' son calls you, be sure
you follow; if what all say who came to Ilium
is true, at the worst you will be a virtuous woman's slave.

CASSANDRA

That servant is a vile thing. Oh, how can heralds keep
their name of honor? Lackeys for despots be they, or   425
lackeys to the people, all men must despise them still.
You tell me that my mother must be slave in the house
of Odysseus? Where are all Apollo's promises
uttered to me, to my own ears, that Hecuba
would die in Troy? What else awaits her—but enough!   430
Poor wretch, he little dreams of what he must go through,
when he will think Troy's pain and mine were golden grace
beside his own luck. Ten years he spent here, and ten
more years will follow before he at last comes home, forlorn°
after the terror of the rock and the thin strait,   435
Charybdis; and the mountain-striding Cyclops, who eats
men's flesh; the Ligyan witch who changes men to swine,
Circe; the wreck of all his ships on the salt sea,
the lotus passion, the sacred oxen of the sun
slaughtered, their dead flesh moaning into speech, to make   440

Odysseus listening shiver. Cut the story short:
he will go down to the water of death, and return alive
to reach his home and thousand sorrows waiting there.

Why must I hurl forth each of Odysseus' labors one by one?
Lead the way quick to the house of death where I shall take
    my mate.   445
Lord of all the sons of Danaus, haughty in your mind of
    pride,
not by day, but evil in the evil night you shall find your grave
when I lie corpse-cold and naked next my husband's
    sepulcher,
piled in the ditch for animals to rip and feed on, beaten by
streaming storms of winter, I who wore Apollo's sacraments.   450
Garlands of the god I loved so well, prophetic spirit's dress,
leave me, as I leave those festivals where once I was so proud.
See, I tear your adornments from my skin not yet defiled
    by touch,
throw them to the running winds to carry off, O lord of
    prophecy.
Where is this general's ship, then? Lead me where I must set
    my feet on board.   455
Wait the wind of favor in the sails; yet when the ship goes out
from this shore, she carries one of the three Furies in my
    shape.
Land of my ancestors, good-bye; O Mother, weep no more
    for me.
You beneath the ground, my brothers, Priam, father of us all,
I will be with you soon and come triumphant to the dead
    below,   460
leaving behind me, wrecked, the house of Atreus, which
    destroyed our house.

        (Exit Cassandra escorted by Talthybius and his
          soldiers to the side. Hecuba collapses.)

Handmaids of aged Hecuba, can you not see
how your mistress, powerless to cry out, lies prone? Oh, take
her hand and help her to her feet, you wretched maids.
Will you let an aged helpless woman lie so long?   465

HECUBA

No. Let me lie where I have fallen. Kind acts, my maids,
must be unkind, unwanted. All that I endure
and have endured and shall, deserves to strike me down.
O gods! What wretched things to call on—gods!—for help
although the decorous action is to invoke their aid   470
when all our hands lay hold on is unhappiness.
No. It is my pleasure first to tell good fortune's tale,
to cast its count more sadly against disasters now.
I was a princess, who was once a prince's bride,
mother by him of sons preeminent, not just   475
mere empty numbers of them, but the lords of the Phrygian
    domain,
such sons for pride to point to as not one woman ever,
no Hellene, none in the wide barbarian world might match.
And then I saw them fall before the spears of Greece,
and cut my hair for them, and laid it on their graves.   480
I mourned their father, Priam. None told me the tale
of his death. I saw it, with these eyes. I stood to watch
his throat cut, at the altar of the protecting god.
I saw my city taken. And the girls I nursed,
choice flowers to wear the pride of any husband's eyes,   485
matured to be dragged by hands of strangers from my arms.
There is no hope left that they will ever see me more,
no hope that I shall ever look on them again.
There is one more stone to key this arch of wretchedness:
I must be carried away to Hellas now, an old   490
slave woman, where all those tasks that wrack old age shall be
given me by my masters. I must work the bolt

that bars their doorway, I whose son was Hector once;
or bake their bread; lay down these withered limbs to sleep
on the bare ground, whose bed was royal once; abuse   495
this skin once delicate the slattern's way, exposed
through robes whose rags will mock my luxury of long since.
Unhappy, O unhappy! And all this came to pass
and shall be, for the way one woman chose a man.

Cassandra, O Daughter, whose inspiration was god-shared,   500
you have paid for your consecration now; at what a price!
And you, my poor Polyxena, where are you now?
Not here, nor any boy or girl of mine, who were
so many once, is near me in my unhappiness.
And you would lift me from the ground? What hope? What
use?   505

(Hecuba rises painfully.)

Guide these feet long ago so delicate in Troy,
a slave's feet now, to the straw sacks laid on the ground
and the piled stones; let me lay down my head and die
in an exhaustion of tears. Of all who walk in bliss
call not one happy yet, until the man is dead.   510

(Hecuba is led to the back of the stage, and
then falls to the ground once more.)

CHORUS [singing]

STROPHE

Voice of singing, stay
with me now, for Ilium's sake;
take up the burden of tears,
new song of sorrow;
the dirge for Troy's death   515
must be chanted;
the tale of my enslavement
by the wheeled stride of the four-foot beast of the Argives,
the horse they left in the gates,
thin gold at its cheeks,   520
inward, the spears' high thunder.

Our people thronging
the rock of Troy roared out the great cry:
"The war is over! Go down,
bring this sacred wood idol   525
to the Maiden of Ilium, Zeus' daughter."
Who stayed then? Not one girl, not one
old man, in their houses,
but singing for happiness
let the lurking death in.   530

ANTISTROPHE

And the generation of Troy
swept solid to the gates
to give the goddess
her pleasure: the horse immortal, unbroken,
the nest of Argive spears,
death for the children of Dardanus   535
sealed in the sleek hill pine chamber.
In the sling of the flax twist, shipwise,
they berthed the black hull
in the shrine of Pallas Athena,   540
stone paved, washed now in the blood of our people.
Strong, joyful work
deep into black night
to the stroke of the Libyan lute
and all Troy singing, and girls'   545
light feet pulsing the air
in joyous dance measures;
indoors, lights everywhere,
torchflares on black
to forbid sleep's onset.   550

EPODE

I was there also: in the great room
I danced for the maiden of the mountains,
Artemis, Zeus' daughter.
Then the cry went up, sudden,   555

bloodshot, up and down the city, to stun
the keep of the citadel. Children
reached shivering hands to clutch
at their mother's dress.
War stalked from his hiding place.   560
Pallas did this.
Beside their altars the Trojans
died in their blood. Desolate now,
men murdered, our sleeping rooms gave up
their brides' beauty   565
to breed sons for Greek men,
sorrow for our own country.

> (Enter Andromache holding Astyanax and sitting in
> a wagon that comes from the side accompanied by
> Greek soldiers and heaped with spoils of war.)

[chanting]
Hecuba look, I see her, rapt
to the enemy wagon, Andromache,
close to whose beating breast clings   570
the boy Astyanax, Hector's sweet child.
O carried away—to what land?—unhappy woman,
on the wagon floor, with the brazen arms
of Hector, of Troy
captive and heaped beside you,
torn now from Troy, for Achilles' son   575
to hang in the shrines of Phthia.

ANDROMACHE [singing in this lyric interchange together with
Hecuba, who sings in reply]

STROPHE A
I go at the hands of Greek masters.

HECUBA
Alas!

ANDROMACHE
            Must the incantation . . .

HECUBA

(*Ah me!*)

ANDROMACHE

. . . of my own grief win tears from you?

HECUBA

It must—O Zeus!

ANDROMACHE

My own distress?   580

HECUBA

O my children . . .

ANDROMACHE

. . . once. No longer.

HECUBA

ANTISTROPHE A

Lost, lost, Troy our dominion . . .

ANDROMACHE

. . . unhappy . . .

HECUBA

. . . and my lordly children.

ANDROMACHE

Gone, alas!

HECUBA

They were mine.

ANDROMACHE

Sorrows only.

HECUBA

Sad destiny . . .   585

ANDROMACHE

. . . of our city . . .

HECUBA

... a wreck, and burning.

ANDROMACHE

Come back, O my husband.°

HECUBA

Poor child, you invoke
a dead man; my son once ...

ANDROMACHE

... my defender.   590

ANDROMACHE

You, who once killed the Greeks ...

HECUBA

... oldest of the sons
I bore to Priam ...

ANDROMACHE

... take me to my death now.

ANDROMACHE

Longing for death drives deep ...

HECUBA

... O sorrowful, such is our fortune ...   595

ANDROMACHE

... lost our city ...

HECUBA

... and our pain lies deep under pain piled over.

ANDROMACHE

We are the hated of the gods, since once your youngest, escaping
death, brought down Troy's towers in the arms of a worthless
woman;

piled at the feet of Pallas the bleeding bodies of our young men
sprawled, kites' food, while Troy takes up the yoke of captivity.   600

HECUBA

ANTISTROPHE C

O my city, my city forlorn . . .

ANDROMACHE

. . . abandoned, I weep this . . .

HECUBA

. . . miserable last hour . . .

ANDROMACHE

. . . of the house where I bore my children.

HECUBA

O my sons, this city and your mother are desolate of you.
Sound of lamentation and sorrow,°
tears on tears shed. Home, farewell.   605
The dead have forgotten all sorrows.

CHORUS LEADER

They who are sad find somehow sweetness in tears, the song
of lamentation and the melancholy Muse.

ANDROMACHE [now speaking]

Hecuba, mother of the man whose spear was death   610
to the Argives, Hector: do you see what they have done to us?

HECUBA [now speaking]

I see the work of gods who pile tower-high the pride
of those who were nothing, and dash present grandeur down.

ANDROMACHE

We are carried away, sad spoils, my boy and I; our life
transformed, we who were noble have now become mere
    slaves.   615

HECUBA

Such is the terror of necessity. I lost
Cassandra, roughly torn from my arms before you came.

[105] THE TROJAN WOMEN

ANDROMACHE

Another Ajax to haunt your daughter? Some such thing
it must be. Yet you have lost still more than you yet know.

HECUBA

There is no numbering my losses. Infinitely   620
misfortune comes to outrace misfortune known before.

ANDROMACHE

Polyxena is dead. They cut your daughter's throat
to pleasure dead Achilles' corpse, above his grave.

HECUBA

O wretched. This was what Talthybius meant, that speech
cryptic, incomprehensible, yet now so clear.   625

ANDROMACHE

I saw her die, and left this wagon seat to lay
a robe upon her body and sing the threnody.

HECUBA

Poor child, poor wretched, wretched darling, sacrificed,
in pain, to a dead man. What monstrous sacrilege!

ANDROMACHE

She is dead, and this was death indeed; and yet to die   630
as she did was happier than to live as I live now.

HECUBA

Child, no. No life, no light is any kind of death,
since death is nothing, and in life the hopes live still.

ANDROMACHE

O Mother, our mother, hear me while I reason through°
this matter fairly—might it even hush your grief!   635
Death, I am sure, is like never being born, but death
is better thus by far than to live a life of pain,
since the dead, with no perception of evil, feel no grief,°
while he who was happy once and then unfortunate
finds his heart driven far from the old lost happiness.   640

She died; it is as if she never saw the light
of day, for she knows nothing now of what she suffered.
But I, who aimed the arrows of ambition high
at honor, and made them good, see now how far I fall,
I, who in Hector's house worked out all custom that brings   645
discretion's name to women. Blame them or blame them not,
there is one act that swings the scandalous speech their way
beyond all else: to leave the house and walk abroad.
I longed to do it, but put the longing aside, and stayed
always within the enclosure of my own house and court.   650
The witty speech some women cultivate I would
not practice, but kept my honest inward thought, and made
my mind my only and sufficient teacher. I gave
my lord's presence the tribute of hushed lips, and eyes
quietly downcast. I knew when my will must have its way   655
over his, knew also how to give way to him in turn.
Men learned of this; I was talked of in the Achaean camp,
and reputation has destroyed me now. At the choice
of women, Achilles' son picked me from the rest, to be
his wife: a murderer's house, and I shall be his slave.   660
If I dash back the beloved memory of Hector
and open wide my heart to my new lord, I shall be
a traitor to the dead love, and know it; if I cling
faithful to the past, I win my master's hatred. Yet
they say one night of love suffices to dissolve   665
a woman's aversion to share the bed of any man.
I hate and loathe that woman who casts away the once
beloved, and takes another in her arms of love.
Even the young mare torn from her running mate and
     teamed
with another will not easily wear the yoke. And yet   670
this is a brute and speechless beast of burden, not
like us intelligent, lower far in nature's scale.
     Dear Hector, when I had you I had a husband, great
in understanding, rank, wealth, courage: all my wish.
I was a virgin when you took me from the house   675

of my father; I gave you all my maiden love, my first,
and now you are dead, and I must cross the sea, to serve,
prisoner of war, the slave's yoke on my neck, in Greece.
No, Hecuba; can you not see my fate is worse
than hers you mourn, Polyxena's? That one thing left   680
always while life lasts, hope, is not for me. I keep
no secret deception in my heart—sweet though it be
to dream—that I shall ever be happy any more.

CHORUS LEADER
You stand where I do in misfortune, and while you mourn
your life, you tell me what I, too, am suffering.   685

HECUBA
I have never been inside the hull of a ship, but know
what I know only by hearsay and from painted scenes,
yet think that seamen, while the gale blows moderately,
take pains to spare unnecessary work, and send
one man to the steering oar, another aloft, and one   690
to pump the bilge from the hold. But when the tempest
    comes
and seas wash over the decks, they lose their nerve, and let
her go by the run at the waves' will, leaving all to chance.
So I, in this succession of disasters, swamped,
battered by this storm immortally inspired, have lost   695
my voice. I hold my tongue and let misfortune go
as it will. Yet still, beloved child, you must forget
what happened with Hector. Tears will never save you now.
Give your obedience to the new master; let your ways
entice his heart to make him love you. If you do   700
it will be better for all who are close to you. This boy,
my own son's child, might grow to manhood and bring
    back—
he alone could do it—something of our city's strength.
On some far day the children of your children might
come home, and build. There still may be another Troy.   705
But *we* say this, and others will speak also. See,

here is some runner of the Achaeans coming now.
Who is he? What news? What counsel have they taken now?

(Enter Talthybius again from the side with his escort.)

TALTHYBIUS

O wife of Hector, once the bravest man in Troy,
do not hate me. This is the will of the Danaans and   710
the kings. I wish I did not have to give this message.

ANDROMACHE

What can this mean, this hint of hateful things to come?

TALTHYBIUS

The council has decreed that your son—how can I say this?

ANDROMACHE

That he shall serve some other master than I serve?

TALTHYBIUS

No man of Achaea shall ever make this boy his slave.   715

ANDROMACHE

Must he be left behind in Phrygia, all alone?

TALTHYBIUS

Worse; horrible. There is no easy way to tell it.

ANDROMACHE

I thank your courtesy—unless your news be really good.

TALTHYBIUS

They will kill your son. It is monstrous. Now you know the
    truth.

ANDROMACHE

Oh, this is worse than anything I heard before.   720

TALTHYBIUS

Odysseus. He urged it before the Greeks, and got his way.

ANDROMACHE

This is too much grief, and more than anyone could bear.

TALTHYBIUS

He said a hero's son could not be allowed to live.

ANDROMACHE

Even thus may his own sons some day find no mercy.

TALTHYBIUS

He must be hurled down from the battlements of Troy.   725
Let it happen this way. It will be wiser in the end.
Do not fight it. Take your grief nobly, as you were born;
give up the struggle where your strength is feebleness
with no force anywhere to help. Listen to me!
Your city is gone, your husband. You are in our power.   730
How can one woman hope to struggle against the arms
of Greece? Think, then. Give up the passionate contest.
                                                        Don't
do any shameful thing, or any deed of hatred.
And please—I request you—hurl no curse at the Achaeans
for fear the army, savage over some reckless word,   735
forbid the child his burial and the dirge of honor.
Be brave, be silent; out of such patience you'll be sure
the child you leave behind will not lie unburied here,
and that to you the Achaeans will be less unkind.

ANDROMACHE

O darling child I loved too well for happiness,   740
your enemies will kill you and leave your mother forlorn.
Your own father's nobility, where others found
protection, means your murder now. The memory
of his valor comes luckless for you. O bridal bed,
O marriage rites that brought me home to Hector's house   745
a bride, you were unhappy in the end. I lived
never thinking the baby I had was born for butchery
by Greeks, but for lordship over all Asia's pride of earth.
Poor child, are you crying too? Do you know what they
will do to you? Your fingers clutch my dress. What use,   750

to nestle like a young bird under the mother's wing?
Hector cannot come back, not burst from underground
to save you, that spear of glory caught in the quick hand,
nor Hector's kin, nor any strength of Phrygian arms.
Yours the sick leap head downward from the height, the fall   755
where none have pity, and the spirit smashed out in death.
O last and loveliest embrace of all, O child's
sweet fragrant body. Vanity in the end. I nursed
for nothing the swaddled baby at this mother's breast;
in vain the wrack of the labor pains and the long weakness.   760
Now once again, and never after this, come close
to your mother, lean against my breast and wind your arms
around my neck, and put your lips against my lips.
Greeks! Your Greek cleverness is simple barbarity.
Why kill this child, who never did you any harm?   765
O flower of the house of Tyndareus! Not his,
not Zeus' daughter, never that, but child of many fathers
I say; the daughter of Vindictiveness, of Hate,
of Blood, Death; of all wickedness that swarms on earth.
I cry it aloud: Zeus never was your father, but you   770
were born a pestilence to all Greeks and the world beside.
Accursed, who from those lovely and accursed eyes
brought down to shame and ruin the bright plains of Troy.
Oh, seize him, take him, dash him to death if it must be done;
feed on his flesh if it is your will. These are the gods   775
who damn us to this death, and I have no strength to save
my boy from execution. Cover my wretched face
and throw me into the ship and that sweet bridal bed
I walk to now across the death of my own child.

(Talthybius lifts the child out of the wagon, which
exits to the side carrying Andromache.)

CHORUS LEADER
Unhappy Troy! For the sweetness in one woman's arms,   780
embrace unspeakable, you lost these thousands slain.

TALTHYBIUS [*chanting*]

Come, boy, taken from the embrace beloved
of your mourning mother. Climb the high circle
of the walls your fathers built. There
end life. This was the order.   785
Take him.

(He hands Astyanax to the guards, who carry him out to the side.)

       I am not the man
to do this. Some other
without pity, not as I ashamed,
should be herald of messages like this.

(Exit to the side.)

HECUBA [*chanting*]

O child of my own unhappy son,   790
shall your life be torn from your mother
and from me? Wicked! Can I help,
dear child, not only suffer? What help?
Tear face, beat bosom. This is all
my power now. O city,   795
O child, what have we left to suffer?
Are we not hurled
down the whole length of disaster?

CHORUS [*singing*]

STROPHE A

Telamon, O king in the land where the bees swarm,
Salamis the surf-pounded isle where you founded your city   800
to front that hallowed coast where Athena broke
forth the primeval pale branch of olive,
wreath of the bright air and a glory on Athens the shining:
O Telamon, you came in your pride of arms
with Alcmene's archer from Greece   805
to Ilium, our city, to sack and destroy it
on that age-old venture.

This was the first flower of Hellenic strength Heracles brought in
  anger
for the horses promised; and by Simois' fair waters   810
checked his surf-wandering oars and made fast the ships' stern
  cables.
From those vessels came out the deadly bow hand,
death to Laomedon, as the scarlet wind of the flames swept over
masonry straight-hewn by the hands of Apollo.   815
This was a desolation of Troy
twice taken; twice in the welter of blood the walls Dardanian
went down before the red spear.

In vain, then, Laomedon's child,   820
you walk in delicate pride
by the golden pitchers
in loveliest servitude
to fill Zeus' wine cups;
while Troy your mother is given to the flame to eat,   825
and the lonely beaches
mourn, as sad birds sing
for the young lost,   830
for the wives and the children
and the aged mothers.
Gone now the shining pools where you bathed,
the fields where you ran
all desolate. And you,
Ganymede, go in grace by the throne of Zeus   835
with your young, calm smile even now
as Priam's kingdom
falls to the Greek spear.   840

O Love, Love, it was you
in the high halls of Dardanus,
the gods were thinking of you,

who greatly glorified Troy
on that day, binding her in marriage   845
with the gods. I speak no more
against Zeus' name.
But the light men love, that shines
through the pale wings of morning,
baleful star for this earth,   850
watched the collapse of Pergamum:
Dawn. Her lord was of this land;
she bore his children,
Tithonus, caught away by the golden car
and the starry horses,   855
who made our hopes so high.
For the gods loved Troy once.
Now they have forgotten.

(*Enter Menelaus from the side, attended by soldiers.*)

MENELAUS

O splendor of sunburst breaking forth this day, whereon   860
I lay my hands once more on Helen, my wife.° And yet
it is not, so much as men think, for a woman's sake
I came to Troy, but against that guest proved treacherous,   865
who like a robber carried the woman from my house.
Since the gods have seen to it that *he* paid the penalty,
fallen before the Hellenic spear, his kingdom wrecked,
I come for *her* now, the Spartan once my own, whose name
I can no longer speak with any happiness,   870
to take her away. In this house of captivity
she is numbered among the other women of Troy, a slave.
And those men whose work with the spear has won her back
gave her to me, to kill, or not to kill, but lead
alive to the land of Argos, if such be my pleasure.   875
And such it is; the death of Helen in Troy I will let
pass, have the oars take her by seaways back to Greek
soil, and there give her over to execution;

blood penalty for friends who are dead in Ilium here.
Go to the house, my followers, and take her out; 880
no, drag her out; lay hands upon that hair so stained
with men's destruction. When the winds blow fair astern
we will take ship again and bring her back to Hellas.

(*Exit several soldiers into the tent.*)

HECUBA

O power, who mount the world, wheel where the world rides,
O mystery of man's knowledge, whosoever you be, 885
named Zeus, nature's necessity or mortal mind,
I call upon you; for you walk the path none hears
yet bring all human action back to right at last.

MENELAUS

What can this mean? How strange a way to call on gods.

HECUBA

Kill your wife, Menelaus, and I will bless your name. 890
But keep your eyes away from her. Desire will win.
She looks enchantment, and where she looks homes are set
    fire;
she captures cities as she captures the eyes of men.
We have had experience, you and I. We know the truth.

(*Enter Helen from the tent escorted by soldiers.*)

HELEN

Menelaus, your first acts are argument of terror 895
to come. Your lackeys put their hands on me. I am dragged
out of my chambers by brute force. I know you hate
me; I am almost sure. And still there is one question
I would ask you, if I may. What have the Greeks decided
to do with me? Or shall I be allowed to live? 900

MENELAUS

You are not strictly condemned, but all the army gave
you into my hands, to kill you for the wrong you did me.

HELEN

Is it permitted that I argue this, and prove
that my death, if I am put to death, will be unjust?

MENELAUS

I did not come to talk with you. I came to kill.   905

HECUBA

No, Menelaus, listen to her. She should not die
unheard. But give me leave to make the opposite case;
the prosecution. There are things that happened in Troy
which you know nothing of, and the long-drawn argument
will mean her death. She never can escape us now.   910

MENELAUS

This is a gift of leisure. Yet if she wants to speak
she may. But it is for your sake, understand, that I give
this privilege I never would have given for her.

HELEN   (To Menelaus.)

Perhaps it will make no difference if I speak
well or badly, and your hate will not let you answer me.   915
All I can do is to foresee the arguments
you will use in accusation of me, and set against
the force of your charges, charges of my own.

                                                First, then!

                                    (Pointing to Hecuba.)

She mothered the beginning of all this wickedness.
For Paris was her child. And next to her the old king,   920
who would not destroy the infant Alexander, that dream
of the firebrand's agony, has ruined Troy and me.
This is not all; listen to the rest I have to say.
Alexander was the judge of the goddess trinity.
Pallas Athena would have given him power, to lead   925
the Phrygian arms on Hellas and make it desolate.
All Asia was Hera's promise, and the uttermost zones

of Europe for his lordship, if her way prevailed.
But Aphrodite, marveling at my loveliness,
promised it to him, if he would say her beauty surpassed   930
all others. Think what this means, and all the consequence.
Cypris prevailed, and I was won in marriage: all
for Greek advantage. You are not ruled by barbarians,
you have not been defeated in war nor serve a tyrant.
Yet Hellas' fortune was my own misfortune. I,   935
sold once for my body's beauty, stand accused, who should
for what has been done wear garlands on my head.

                                                 I know.
You will say all this is nothing to the immediate charge:
I did run away; I did go secretly from your house.
But when he came to me—call him any name you will: 940
Paris? or Alexander? that ruinous spirit sent
to haunt this woman—he came with a goddess at his side,
no weak one. And you—it was criminal—took ship for Crete
and left me there in Sparta in the house, alone.

                                          You see?
I wonder—and I ask this of myself, not you—   945
why *did* I do it? What made me run away from home
with the stranger, and betray my country and my hearth?
Challenge the goddess then; show your strength greater than
     Zeus'
who has the other gods in his power, and still is slave
to Aphrodite alone! Shall I not be forgiven?   950
Still you might have some show of argument against me.
When Paris was gone to the deep places of death, below
ground, and my marriage given by the gods was gone,
I should have come back to the Argive ships, left Troy.
I did try to do it, and I have witnesses,   955
the towers' gatekeepers and the sentinels on the wall,
who caught me again and again as I let down the rope
from the battlements and tried to slip away to the ground.
As for Deiphobus, my second husband: he took me away°
by force and kept me his wife against the Phrygians' will.   960

O my husband, can you kill me now and think you kill
in righteousness?° I was the bride of force. Besides,
my natural beauty brought me the sorrow of slavery
instead of victory. Would you be stronger than the gods?
Try, then. But any such ambition is absurd.   965

CHORUS LEADER
O Queen of Troy, stand by your children and your country!
Break down the beguilement of this woman, since she speaks
well, but has done wickedly. This is dangerous.

HECUBA
First, to defend the honor of the gods, and show
that the woman is a scandalous liar. I will not   970
believe it! Hera and the virgin Pallas Athena
could never be so silly and empty-headed
that Hera would sell Argos to the barbarians,
or Pallas let Athenians be the slaves of Troy.
They went to Ida in girlish emulation, vain   975
of their own loveliness? Why? Tell me the reason Hera
should fall so much in love with the idea of beauty.
To win some other lord more powerful than Zeus?
Or had Athena marked some god to be her mate,
she, whose virginity is a privilege won from Zeus,   980
she who abjures marriage? Do not trick out your own sins
by calling the gods stupid. No wise man will believe you.
You claim, and I must laugh to hear it, that Aphrodite
came at my son's side to the house of Menelaus?
She could have caught up you and your city of Amyclae   985
and set you in Ilium, moving not from the quiet of heaven!
Nonsense. My son was handsome beyond all other men.
You looked at him, and sense went Cyprian at the sight,
since Aphrodite is nothing but the human lust,
named rightly, since the word of lust begins the god's name.°   990
You saw him in the barbaric splendor of his robes,
gorgeous with gold. It made your senses itch. You thought,
being queen only in Argos, in little luxury,

that once you got rid of Sparta for the Phrygian city
where gold streamed everywhere, you could let extravagance   995
run wild. No longer were Menelaus and his house
sufficient for your spoiled luxurious appetites.
So much for that. You say my son took you away
by force. What Spartan heard you cry for help? You did
cry out? Or did you? Castor, your brother, was there, a young   1000
man, and his twin not yet caught up among the stars.
Then when you had reached Troy, and the Argives at your
    heels
came, and the agony of the murderous spears began,
when the reports came in that Menelaus' side
was winning, you would praise him, simply to make my son   1005
unhappy at the strength of his love's challenger,
forgetting your husband when the luck went back to Troy.
You worked hard: not to make yourself a better woman,
but to make sure always to be on the winning side.
You claim you tried to slip away with ropes let down   1010
from the ramparts, and this proves you stayed against your
    will?
Perhaps. But when were you ever caught in the strangling
    noose,
or sharpening a dagger? Which any noble wife
would do, desperate with longing for her lord's return.
Yet over and over again I gave you good advice: 1015
"Make your escape, my daughter; there are other girls
for my sons to marry. I will help you get away
to the ships of the Achaeans. Let the Greeks, and us,
stop fighting." So I argued, but you were not pleased.
Spoiled in the luxury of Alexander's house   1020
you liked foreigners to kiss the ground before your feet.
All that impressed you.

                              And now you dare to come outside,
figure fastidiously arranged, to look upon
the same sky as your husband, O abominable
heart, who should walk submissively in rags of robes,   1025

shivering with anxiety, head Scythian-cropped,
your old impudence gone and modesty gained at last
with reference to your sinful life.
                                        O Menelaus,
mark this, the end of my argument. Be true to your
high reputation and to Hellas. Grace both, and kill   1030
Helen. Thus make it the custom toward all womankind
hereafter, that the price of adultery is death.

CHORUS LEADER

Menelaus, keep the ancestral honor of your house.
Punish your wife, and clear your name of the accusation
of cowardice. You shall seem great even to your enemies.   1035

MENELAUS

All you have said falls into line with my own thought.
This woman left my household for a stranger's bed
of her own free will, and all this talk of Aphrodite
is for pure show. Away, and face the stones of the mob.
Atone for the long labors of the Achaeans in   1040
the brief act of dying, and know your penance for my shame.

                    (Helen falls before him and embraces his knees.)

HELEN

No, by your knees! I am not guilty of the mind's
infection, which the gods sent. Do not kill! Have pity!

HECUBA

Be true to the memory of all your friends she murdered.
It is for them and for their children that I plead.   1045

                            (Menelaus pushes Helen away.)

MENELAUS

Enough, Hecuba. I am not listening to her now.
I speak to my servants: see that she is taken away
to where the ships are beached. She will make the voyage
    home.

HECUBA

But let her not be put in the same ship with you.

MENELAUS

What can you mean? That she is heavier than she was?   1050

HECUBA

A man in love once never is out of love again.

MENELAUS

Sometimes; when the beloved's heart turns false to him.
Yet it shall be as you wish. She shall not be allowed
in the same ship I sail in. This was well advised.
And once in Argos she must die the vile death earned   1055
by her vile life, and be an example to all women
to live temperately. This is not the easier way;
and yet her execution will tincture with fear
the lust of women even more depraved than she.

(Exit Menelaus and Helen to the side escorted by soldiers.)

CHORUS [*singing*]

STROPHE A

Thus, O Zeus, you betrayed all   1060
to the Achaeans: your temple
in Ilium, your misted altar,
the flame of the clotted sacraments,
the smoke of the skying incense,
Pergamum the hallowed,   1065
the ivied ravines of Ida, washed
by the running snow, the utter
peaks that surprise the sun bolts,
shining and primeval place of divinity.   1070

ANTISTROPHE A

Gone are your sacrifices, the choirs'
glad voices singing, for the gods
night long festivals in the dark;
gone the images, gold on wood

laid, the twelves of the sacred moons,   1075
the magic Phrygian number.
Can it be, can it be, my lord, you have forgotten,
from your throne high in heaven's
bright air, my city which is ruined
and the flame storm that broke it?   1080

O my dear, my husband, O wandering ghost
unwashed, unburied; the sea hull must carry me   1085
in the flash of its wings' speed
to Argos, city of horses, where
the stone walls built by giants invade the sky.
The multitudes of our children stand
clinging to the gates and cry through their tears.
And one girl weeps:°   1090
"O Mother, the Achaeans take me away
lonely from your eyes
to the black ship
where the oars dip surf   1095
toward Salamis the blessed,
or the peak between two seas
where Pelops' castle
keeps the gates at the Isthmus."

Oh that as Menelaus' ship   1100
makes way through the mid-sea
the bright pronged spear immortal of thunder might smash it
far out in the Aegean,
as in tears, in bondage to Hellas,   1105
I am cut from my country;
as she holds the golden mirror
in her hands, girls' grace,
she, Zeus' daughter.
Let him never come home again, to a room in Laconia   1110
and the hearth of his fathers;

never more to Pitana's streets
and the bronze gates of Athena;
since he possesses his shame
and the vile marriage, the sorrows   1115
of great Hellas and the land
watered by Simois.

> *(Enter Talthybius again from the side, accompanied by soldiers*
> *who carry the body of Astyanax, laid on the shield of Hector.)*

[chanting]
But see!
New evils multiply in our land.
Behold, O pitiful wives
of the Trojans. This is Astyanax,   1120
dead, dashed without pity from the walls, and borne
by the Danaans, who murdered him.

TALTHYBIUS
Hecuba, one last ship, that of Achilles' son,
remains, manned at the oar sweeps now, to carry back
to the shores of Phthiotis his last spoils of war.   1125
Neoptolemus himself has put to sea. He heard
news of old Peleus in difficulty and his land
invaded by Acastus, son of Pelias.
Such news put speed above all pleasure of delay.
So he is gone, and took with him Andromache,   1130
whose lamentations for her country and farewells
to Hector's tomb as she departed brought these tears
crowding into my eyes. And she implored that we
bury this dead child, your own Hector's son, who died
flung from the battlements of Troy. She asked as well   1135
that the bronze-backed shield, terror of the Achaeans once,
when the boy's father slung its defense across his side,
be not taken to the hearth of Peleus, nor the room
where the slain child's Andromache must be a bride
once more, to waken memories by its sight, but used°   1140

in place of the cedar coffin and stone-chambered tomb
for the boy's burial. He shall be laid in your arms
to wrap the body about with winding sheets, and flowers,
as well as you can, out of that which is left to you.
For she is gone. Her master's speed prevented her   1145
from giving the rites of burial to her little child.

The rest of us, once the corpse is laid out, and earth
is piled above it, must raise the mast tree, and go.
Do therefore quickly everything that you must do.
There is one labor I myself have spared you. As   1150
we forded on our way here Scamander's running water,
I washed the body and made clean the wounds. I go
now, to break ground and dig the grave for him, that my
work be made brief, as yours must be, and our tasks end
together, and the ships be put to sea, for home.   1155

HECUBA
Lay down the circled shield of Hector on the ground:
a hateful thing to look at; it means no love to me.

(Exit Talthybius and his escort to the side.)

Achaeans! All your strength is in your spears, not in
the mind. What were you afraid of, that it made you kill
this child so savagely? That Troy, which fell, might be   1160
raised from the ground once more? Your strength meant
    nothing, then.
When Hector's spear was fortunate, and numberless
strong hands were there to help him, we were still destroyed.
Now when the city is fallen and the Phrygians slain,
this baby terrified you? I despise the fear   1165
which is pure terror in a mind unreasoning.

O darling child, how wretched was this death! You might
have fallen fighting for your city, grown to man's
age, and married, and with the king's power like a god's,

and died happy, if there is any happiness here.   1170
But no. You grew to where you could see and learn, my child,
yet your life was not old enough to win advantage
of fortune. How wickedly, poor boy, your fathers' walls,
Apollo's handiwork, have shorn your pitiful curls
tended and trimmed to ringlets by your mother's hand,   1175
and the face she kissed once, where the brightness now is
    blood
shining through the torn bones—too horrible to say more.
O little hands, sweet likenesses of Hector's once,
now you lie broken at the wrists before my feet;
and mouth beloved whose words were once so confident,   1180
you are dead; and all was false, when you would jump into
my bed, and say: "Grandmother, when you die I will cut
my long hair in your memory, and at your grave
bring companies of boys my age, to sing farewell."
It did not happen; now I, a homeless, childless, old   1185
woman must bury your poor corpse, which is so young.
Alas for all the tendernesses, my nursing care,
and our shared slumbers gone. What would the poet say,
what words might he inscribe upon your monument?
"Here lies a little child the Argives killed, because   1190
they were afraid of him." That? The epitaph of Greek shame.
You will not win your father's heritage, except
for this, which is your coffin now: the brazen shield.

O shield, that guarded the strong shape of Hector's arm:
the bravest man of all, who wore you once, is dead.   1195
How sweet the impression of his body on your sling,
and at the true circle of your rim the stain of sweat
where in the grind of his many combats Hector leaned
his chin against you, and the drops fell from his brow!

Take up your work now; bring from what is left some fair   1200
coverings to wrap this poor dead child. The gods will not
allow us much. But let him have what we can give.

That mortal is a fool who, prospering, thinks his life
has any strong foundation; since our fortune's course
of action is the reeling way a madman takes,   1205
and no one person is ever happy all the time.

> *(Hecuba's handmaidens bring out a robe and ornaments from the*
> *tent and help Hecuba prepare the body of Astyanax for burial.)*

CHORUS LEADER
Here are your women, who bring you from the Trojan spoils
what is left, to deck the corpse for burial.

HECUBA
O child, it is not for victory in riding, won
from boys your age, not archery—in which acts our people   1210
take pride, without driving competition to excess°—
that your sire's mother lays upon you now these treasures
from what was yours before; though now the god-accursed,
Helen, has robbed you, she who has destroyed as well
the life in you, and brought to ruin all our house.   1215

CHORUS [*singing in this interchange with Hecuba, who for the most*
part replies speaking]
  My heart,
  you touched my heart, you who were once
  a great lord in my city.°

HECUBA [*speaking*]
These Phrygian robes' magnificence you should have worn
at your marriage to some princess uttermost in pride
in all the East. I lay them on your body now.   1220
And you, once so victorious and mother of
a thousand conquests, Hector's huge beloved shield:
here is a wreath for you, who die not, yet are dead
with this body; since it is better far to honor you
than the armor of Odysseus the wicked and clever.   1225

CHORUS
Ah me.

Earth takes you, child;
our tears of sorrow.
Cry aloud, our mother.

HECUBA [*singing*]
Yes.

CHORUS
The dirge of the dead.

HECUBA [*singing*]
Ah me.   1230

CHORUS
Evils never to be forgotten.

HECUBA [*speaking*]
I'll bind some of your wounds with bandages, and be
your healer: a wretched one, in name alone, no use.
Among the dead your father will take care of the others.

CHORUS
Rip, tear your faces with hands   1235
that beat like oars.
Alas.

HECUBA
Dear women. . . .

CHORUS
Hecuba, speak to us. We are yours.° What did you cry aloud?

HECUBA
The gods meant nothing° except to make life hard for me,   1240
and of all cities they chose Troy to hate. In vain
we sacrificed. And yet had not the very hand
of a god gripped and crushed this city deep in the ground,
we should have disappeared in darkness, and not given
a theme for music, and the songs of men to come.   1245
You may go now, and hide the dead in his poor tomb;
he has those flowers that are the right of the underworld.

I think it makes small difference to the dead, if they
are buried in the tokens of luxury. All that
is an empty glorification left for those who live.   1250

(The body of Astyanax is carried off to the side.)

CHORUS [*singing*]
Sad mother, whose hopes were so huge
for your life. They are broken now.
Born to high blessedness
and a lordly line, child,
your death was horror.   1255

But see, see
on the high places of Ilium
the torchflares whirling in the hands
of men. For Troy
some other new agony.

(Enter Talthybius with soldiers from the side.)

TALTHYBIUS
I call to the captains who have orders to set fire   1260
to the city of Priam: keep no longer in the hand
the shining flame. Let loose the fire upon it. So
with the citadel of Ilium broken to the ground
we can take leave of Troy, in gladness, and go home.

I speak to you, too, for my orders include this,   1265
daughters of Troy. When the lords of the armament sound
the high echoing crash of the trumpet call, then go
to the ships of the Achaeans, to be taken away
from this land. And you, unhappiest and aged woman,
go with them. For Odysseus' men are here, to whom   1270
enslaved the lot exiles you from your native land.

HECUBA
Ah, wretched me. So this is the unhappy end
and goal of all the sorrows I have lived. I go

forth from my country and a city lit with flames.
Come, aged feet; make one last weary struggle, that I 1275
may hail my city in its affliction. O Troy, once
so huge over all Asia in the drawn wind of pride,
your very name of glory shall be stripped away.
They are burning you, and us they drag forth from our land
enslaved. O gods! Do I call upon the gods for help? 1280
We cried to them before now, and they would not hear.
Come then, hurl ourselves into the pyre. Best now
to die in the flaming ruins of our fathers' house!

TALTHYBIUS

Unhappy creature, ecstatic in your sorrows! Men,
take her, don't wait. She is Odysseus' property. 1285
You have orders to deliver her into his hands.

HECUBA [*singing, with the Chorus also singing in reply*]
STROPHE A

O sorrow.
Cronion, Zeus, lord of Phrygia,
prince of our house, have you seen
the dishonor done to the seed of Dardanus?° 1290

CHORUS

He has seen, but the great city
is a city no more, it is gone. There is no Troy.

HECUBA

ANTISTROPHE A

O sorrow.
Ilium flares. 1295
The chambers of Pergamum take fire,
the citadel and the wall's high places.

CHORUS

Our city fallen to the spear
fades as smoke winged in the sky,

halls hot in the swept fire°   1300
and the fierce lances.

HECUBA

O soil where my children grew.

CHORUS
Alas.

HECUBA
O children, hear me; it is your mother who calls.

CHORUS
They are dead you cry to. This is a dirge.

HECUBA
I lean my old body against the earth   1305
and both hands beat the ground.

CHORUS
I kneel to the earth, take up
the cry to my own dead,
poor buried husband.

HECUBA
We are taken, dragged away . . .

CHORUS
                                   . . . a cry of pain, pain . . .   1310

HECUBA
. . . under the slave's roof . . .

CHORUS
                                   . . . away from my country.

HECUBA
Priam, my Priam. Dead,
graveless, forlorn,
you know not what they have done to me.

CHORUS

Now dark, holy death   1315
in the brutal butchery closed his eyes.

HECUBA

ANTISTROPHE B

O gods' house, city beloved . . .

CHORUS

. . . alas . . .

HECUBA

. . . you are given the red flame and the spear's iron.

CHORUS

You will collapse to the dear ground and be nameless.

HECUBA

Ash as the skyward smoke wing   1320
piled will blot from my sight the house where I lived once.

CHORUS

Lost shall be the name of the land,
all gone, perished. Troy, city of sorrow,
is there no longer.

                                                    (A loud crash is heard.)

HECUBA

Did you see, did you hear?

CHORUS

                                        The crash of the citadel.   1325

HECUBA

The earth shook, riven . . .

CHORUS

                                        . . . to engulf the city.

HECUBA

O

shaking, tremulous limbs,
this is the way. Forward:
into the slave's life.   1330

CHORUS

Mourn for the ruined city, then go away
to the ships of the Achaeans.

                                              (Exit all.)

IPHIGENIA AMONG THE TAURIANS

Translated by ANNE CARSON

IPHIGENIA AMONG THE TAURIANS: INTRODUCTION

The Play: Date and Composition

There is no external evidence available for determining when Euripides' *Iphigenia among the Taurians* was first produced. Scholars date it to 414–13 BCE on the basis of various metrical features. The play is strikingly similar to *Helen*, which is known to have been produced in 412 BCE, and it seems unlikely that Euripides would have staged two such similar plays in the very same year. Presumably Euripides wrote *Iphigenia* for the annual competition at the Great Dionysian Festival in Athens. What the other three plays were in Euripides' tetralogy of that year, and how they fared in the competition, are unknown.

The play is often called *Iphigenia in Tauris*, but there was never any country or physical region called Tauris; the Taurians or Tauri were a primitive, warlike people who lived on the Crimean peninsula on the northern coast of the Black Sea, and the Greek title of the play designates Iphigenia as being "among" these people (as does the Latin title *Iphigenia in Tauris*). Euripides probably originally titled his play simply *Iphigenia*, and the further specification was added when it was included in a complete edition of his works (perhaps around the third century BCE) in order to distinguish it from his *Iphigenia in Aulis*.

The Myth

Iphigenia among the Taurians presents one of the final episodes of the tragic vicissitudes of the house of Atreus, the royal dynasty of Argos (or Mycenae): Agamemnon, his wife Clytemnestra, her lover Aegisthus, and her children Iphigenia, Electra, and Orestes. According to the version of the myth that Euripides presupposes, Iphigenia, who all the Greeks thought had been sacrificed by her father at Aulis at the beginning of the Trojan War, was in fact rescued by Artemis and transported to the land of the Taurians. There she has become a priestess of Artemis and participates in the local ritual whereby any foreigners who arrive, especially Greeks, are sacrificed to the goddess. Meanwhile, her brother Orestes, who was just a child at the time of the events at Aulis, has grown up and killed his mother to avenge her murder of his father, and is consequently being pursued by Furies (some of whom have continued to torment him even after he was acquitted at a trial in Athens). Now Apollo has prophesied to Orestes that, if he brings back to Greece the cult statue of Artemis from the land of the Taurians, he will finally be cleansed of his guilt and cured of his sufferings.

It is at this point that the action of Euripides' play begins. Orestes and his comrade Pylades arrive by ship in the land of the Taurians but are captured and brought to the temple to be killed. Not knowing who they are, Iphigenia is just about to sacrifice one or both of them—both Orestes and Pylades demonstrate extraordinary nobility and generosity by each offering to die so that the other can be saved—but a complex and suspenseful scene leads surprisingly to the brother's and sister's recognition of each other. In the second half of the play, Iphigenia devises an escape for all three of them: she pretends that the cult statue has been polluted by contact with matricides and must be cleansed in the sea, and the three Greeks manage to flee with it but become embroiled in a battle with the Taurians on the beach. At the end, Athena appears so that she can placate Thoas, the king of the Taurians, and foretell the future: Orestes must bring the statue to Halae in Attica, founding a ritual in which a man's throat will merely be scratched by a sword to draw a little blood; and Iphigenia will become a priestess at the Greek cult center of Artemis at Brauron, also in Attica.

The episode dramatized in Euripides' *Iphigenia among the Taurians* belongs to one of the most popular sets of stories in all of Greek tragedy. Euripides himself returned repeatedly to this mythic complex to treat other tales from it, in such plays as *Electra* (written ca. 420 BCE), *Orestes* (408 BCE), and *Iphigenia in Aulis* (produced posthumously after 406 BCE). But while the other episodes of the history of the sons of Atreus were dramatized by many other tragedians, including Aeschylus (in the *Oresteia*) and Sophocles (in his *Electra*), Euripides' selection of this particular story and his treatment of it seem to have been entirely unprecedented.

Euripides drew upon three different kinds of material in creating this play: regional religious cults, poetic narratives, and historiography.

- The cult of the goddess Artemis and her priestess Iphigenia at Brauron celebrated fertility and protected reproduction and the young, especially among women. By contrast, the cult of Artemis Tauropolos at Halae seems to have focused somewhat more upon male coming-of-age. Both cults were well established and certainly familiar to most members of the original audience, but the link between the cults and the legendary stories about the children of Agamemnon was presumably much less clear.
- In Greek legend and early poetry, Iphigenia was either killed at Aulis or else (the usual version) she was rescued by Artemis and made immortal. In this play she is indeed saved and conveyed to the Taurians, but she remains fully mortal, a human counterpart to the goddess Artemis: each of them is out of place among this savage race and needs to be rescued by her brother and brought back to the civilization of Greece. So too, Orestes' pollution from killing his mother and his persecution by the Furies were familiar elements of Greek myth, lyric poetry, and tragedy (most notably in Aeschylus' *Oresteia*), but Euripides has innovated boldly in the myth so as to bring Orestes to the land of the Taurians and have him meet Iphigenia there.

- Besides these religious and mythical dimensions, Euripides' tragedy also makes use of recent ethnographic field reporting. Only a couple of decades before this play was composed, the historian Herodotus had provided a detailed description of the Taurians as a savage and bloodthirsty race who sacrificed Greeks and shipwrecked mariners to a goddess they identified as Iphigenia. The general characteristics and many details of the Taurians described by Herodotus recur emphatically in Euripides' play.

Out of all these disparate elements, with characteristic panache and pathos, Euripides has contrived one of his most brilliant and gripping dramas. In particular, the elements of pathetic misunderstanding, mistaken identities, and last-minute recognition, clever Greeks escaping from stupid barbarians, miraculous guidance and intervention by the gods, and an unexpected "happy ending" after a seemingly interminable series of disasters for this long-suffering family, mark this play as a perfect example (along with *Ion, Helen,* and other plays now lost) of the "romantic" type of tragedy, in contrast to the more common plot structure that ends in disaster and death for the main characters.

Transmission and Reception

Iphigenia among the Taurians seems to have been one of Euripides' more popular plays in antiquity. Aristophanes parodies it in at least two of his comedies; Aristotle discusses it repeatedly in the *Poetics* to illustrate how a recognition scene should be constructed; and later Greek and Latin authors frequently refer to the play, alluding particularly to its portrayal of the exemplary friendship between Orestes and Pylades. We know from an inscription that the play was performed at the Great Dionysian Festival in 341 BCE and won a prize. Further testimony to its ancient popularity comes from a dozen Attic and south Italic vases of the fourth century BCE (all focus on the first half of the play) and from Pompeian wall frescoes of the first century CE and Roman sarcophagi of the second century CE—these show later scenes as well. Finally, at least four papyri with parts of the play have been discovered; they range from the third century BCE to the fourth century CE.

But for some reason we do not know, *Iphigenia among the Taurians* was not one of the canonical ten plays selected for more intense study and wider diffusion. It survived antiquity only by the accident of being among the so-called alphabetic plays (see "Introduction to Euripides," p. 3), and it is transmitted by a single manuscript (and its copies) and is not accompanied by the ancient commentaries (scholia) that explain various kinds of interpretative difficulties.

The standard story of Iphigenia's sacrifice at Aulis has always fascinated authors and artists and has tended to be even more popular than Euripides' innovative account of her survival and of her and Orestes' adventures among the Taurians. But in the world of Renaissance colonialism the adventures of brave young Europeans among exotic savages acquired new topicality, while the noble self-sacrifice of the two friends Orestes and Pylades displayed virtues that were not only pagan. Both themes inspired tragedians as early as Giovanni Rucellai (*L'Oreste*, 1525) and painters as late as Anselm Feuerbach (1862). Jean Racine planned an *Iphigénie en Tauride* (1673–76?) but never wrote it; only an outline of the first act survives. But the high point of the reception of Euripides' play was the eighteenth century, among painters like Giovanni Battista Tiepolo (1736), Benjamin West (1766), and Henry Fuseli; tragedians like John Dennis (*Iphigenia*, 1699), Johann Elias Schlegel (*Die Geschwister in Taurien*, 1739; revised as *Orest und Pylades*, 1742), and Claude Guimond de La Touche (*Iphigénie en Tauride*, 1757); and composers of operas like Domenico Scarlatti (*Ifigenia in Tauri*, 1713). The two greatest adaptations both date from 1779: Christoph Willibald Gluck's opera *Iphigénie en Tauride* and Johann Wolfgang Goethe's drama *Iphigenie auf Tauris* (revised 1787). Both these Enlightenment texts humanize and ennoble the Euripidean original, transforming a suspenseful and rather racy stage play into an exploration of universal human emotions and a document of philanthropy. They have also dominated the subsequent reception of the play, even in music (Franz Schubert, "Orest auf Tauris" and "Iphigenia," 1817) and comic opera (Eugène Scribe, *Oreste et Pylade*, 1844). Noteworthy interpretations in the twentieth century include dance dramas by Isadora Duncan (1916) and Pina Bausch (1974), a poem by Randall Jarrell ("Orestes at Tauris," 1936), and a drama by the German author Egon Fritz (*Iphigenie in Amerika*, 1948).

IPHIGENIA AMONG THE TAURIANS

Characters   IPHIGENIA, daughter of Agamemnon and
Clytemnestra; priestess of Artemis
ORESTES, son of Agamemnon and
Clytemnestra
PYLADES, friend of Orestes
CHORUS of captive Greek women
TAURIAN HERDSMAN
THOAS, king of the Taurians
MESSENGER, a servant of Thoas
ATHENA

*Scene: The entrance to the temple of Artemis in the land of the
Taurians, with a large, bloodstained altar in front of it.*

(Enter Iphigenia from the temple.)

IPHIGENIA

Pelops son of Tantalus came to Pisa on swift horses
and married Oenomaus' daughter
who begot Atreus.
Atreus begot Menelaus and Agamemnon.
Agamemnon begot me.
I am Iphigenia, daughter of the daughter of Tyndareus.   5
My father killed me—
at Euripus where stiff breezes
spin the salt-blue sea in spirals,
for Helen's sake

a sacrifice to Artemis in famous Aulis—
or so people think.

        For at Aulis Agamemnon   10
had assembled a thousand ships,
a Greek expedition to take the crown of Troy.
He wanted the Greeks to avenge Helen's rape
and gratify Menelaus.
What befell him was the disaster of windlessness.
He resorted to divination
and Calchas said this: 15
"Agamemnon, commander of this Greek army,
not one ship will cast off from this shore
until Artemis receives your own girl
Iphigenia
as a sacrifice.
You made a vow once   20
to Artemis Lightbringer to offer up
the finest fruit of that year
and that year
your wife bore a child in the house—"
that "finest fruit" was me!
"Her you must kill."

        So Odysseus planned it:
they got me from my mother on pretext of marrying Achilles.   25
And I came to Aulis—sad day for me!
Lifted high above the altar I was right on the verge of death
when Artemis snatched me,
put a deer in my place.
Sent me clear through the air to the land of the Taurians: here!   30
The land is barbarian, so is the king—Thoas
(his name means "swift" and he is).
The goddess put me here in her temple as priestess.
And there's a ritual°   35
beautiful in name only,
that Artemis finds pleasing—well,

I won't say more. She terrifies me.
The fact is, by a law of the city older than me
I sacrifice any Greek man who comes here.
That is, I start things off. Others do the killing.   40
Inside the temple.
We don't talk about this.

New strange dreams came in the night.
I shall tell them—it might bring relief.
In my dream it seemed I'd gone from this land to live in
    Argos.   45
I was lying asleep in a room of girls
when the earth gave a jolt.
I fled, stood outside, saw the cornice falling
and the whole roof collapse to the ground in a heap.
One pillar remained of our ancestral home: 50
I saw it grow blonde hair and speak a human voice.
Then putting my stranger-killing skills to use
I began sprinkling water
as on one about to die.
And I was weeping.
Here's how I read this dream: 55
Orestes is dead, it was him I sprinkled with water.
Boys are the pillars of a house, are they not,
and anyone I consecrate does die.°
So I want to offer libations to my brother.   60
He and I are far apart
but this at least I can do.
I'll go with my women—Greeks given me by the king.
For some reason they're not here yet.
I shall go into the temple—that's where I live.   65

(Exit Iphigenia into the temple.
Enter Orestes and Pylades from the side.)

ORESTES
    Look, be careful. Might be someone on the path.

PYLADES

Yes, I'm peering in every direction.

ORESTES

Pylades, does this look to you like the goddess' temple,
the one we sailed here from Argos to find?   70

PYLADES

Yes it does, Orestes.

ORESTES

And this is the altar, wet with Greek blood?

PYLADES

The top of it anyway is bloodstained red.

ORESTES

And do you see spoils hanging from the top?

PYLADES

Spoils from foreigners who died here.   75
But I think I should take a good look around.

ORESTES

O Phoebus, what is this net you have led me into?
Your oracle bid me avenge my father's blood
by killing my mother
but relays of Furies
came hounding me from my land   80
and after I'd run lap after lap on their turning track
I came to you, asked how to find my way out
of wheeling madness and pain.°
You told me to go to the Taurian land   85
where your sister Artemis has her altars
and steal a statue of the goddess
that (people say) fell from the sky to this temple here.
Take it by cunning or take it by luck, no matter the risk,   90
and give it to Athens.
That's all you said.

If I do this, I breathe free.
So
I obeyed you, I came here.
To a land unknown and inhospitable.
But, Pylades, tell me, what should we do?   95
You're my partner in this.
You see those high encircling walls?
Should we mount ladders?
But won't we be seen? Or force the bolts with crowbars?°
But we know of no crowbars.
And if we're caught opening the gates   100
or devising a way in, we're dead.
Let's just run for it, before we get killed—
we can use the same boat we came on.

PYLADES
To run is unacceptable. We're not like that.
And the oracle of god must be respected.   105
Let's quit this temple and go hide in the caves
where the dark seawater washes in.
We'll keep our distance from the ship
in case someone sees it, reports us and has us arrested.
And as soon as the eye of night darkens   110
we must nerve ourselves to steal that statue from the temple
any way we can.°
Good men find the nerve for ordeals, cowards are nothing.°   115

ORESTES
You're right, yes, we should hide out somewhere.
It won't be my fault if the god's oracle goes unfulfilled.   120
We will find the nerve!
Young men have no excuse shirking hard work!

(Exit Orestes and Pylades to one side. Enter the Chorus
of captive Greek women from the other side.)

CHORUS° [*singing*]
Silence!

O you who dwell by the Clashing Rocks and the Hostile Sea!   125
O Dictynna,
child of Leto, wild as mountains,
to your court, to your gold columns I come,
a pure holy girl on pure holy feet,   130
serving the one who holds your holy key,
I who have lost the towers and walls of Greece rich in horses,
lost the groves and grasslands of Europe,   135
lost the halls of my father,
here I am.
Tell me your news, tell me your troubles.
Why have you brought me, brought me to the temple,
O child of the man
who came against the towers of Troy
with a glorious fleet of a thousand ships
and ten thousand glorious men?°   140

(Enter Iphigenia from the temple.)

IPHIGENIA [singing in this lyric interchange with the Chorus, who
continue to sing in reply]
My ladies!
I'm oppressed by the pain of lament,   145
by lyreless unmusical music,
by keening.
Ruin comes at me.
I grieve for my brother—
such a vision I saw in the night just past.°   150
I am lost.
Am lost.
Our house is no more.
Our family gone.   155
What sorrows swept Argos!
O god, you god,
who rob me of my only brother
by sending him down to death.
For him I pour out these libations

and a mixing bowl to wet the earth—   160
milk of mountain cows,
wine of Bacchus,
honey of yellow bees,
these I pour.
They comfort the dead.   165

Now hand me that vessel of gold,
libation for the god of death.

O child of Agamemnon under the ground,   170
these are for you.
Receive them.
I'll not be bringing bright locks of hair to crown your tomb,
I'll not be bringing tears.
I am far far away from our homeland, yours and mine,   175
and the people there think I am butchered and dead.

CHORUS
   Mistress,
   I'll sing you antiphonies,
   the rough raw noise of Asian songs,   180
   dirges for the dead—
   what Hades sings—the opposite of paeans.   185
   Pity the house of Atreus!
   Gone is its light, its scepter.
   Gone is the pomp of all those brilliant kings.°   190
   Trouble rushes on trouble.
   One day in a whirl of winged horses
   the Sun changed course
   and turned his holy face away.
   Then sorrow upon sorrow came to the house of the golden lamb,   195
   killing on killing, grief on grief:
   from all that ancient Tantalid wrong   200
   punishment unfolds now.
   And the god is zealous against you.

IPHIGENIA

From the beginning my luck was unlucky.°
Right from my mother's womb, that first night,   205
the Fates wove an absolute education for me.
I was the firstborn of Leda's poor daughter,   210
victim of a father's atrocity,
an offering that brought no joy.°
They rode me in chariots over Aulis' sands—   215
a bride!
Pity me—I was no bride! Bride of Achilles,
alas!
Now I live as a stranger in a barren house by the Hostile Sea.
I've no marriage, no children, no city, no loved ones.   220
Once the Greeks wooed me.°   208
I no longer sing songs for Hera at Argos,   221
I no longer weave Athenas and Titans
to the hum of the loom.
No, I work in blood—making death for strangers°   225
who cry out for pity, who shed tears for pity.
I give not a thought to them now.   230
It's my brother I weep, killed in Argos.
Him I left a mere infant,
a baby, a young thing, a tendril in his mother's hands,
at his mother's breast:
the rightful scepter-bearing king of Argos, Orestes.   235

(Enter Herdsman from the side.)

CHORUS LEADER

But look, here comes a herdsman
heading up from the shore with news for you.

HERDSMAN

Child of Agamemnon and Clytemnestra,
listen to my strange report.

IPHIGENIA [*now speaking*]

What strange report?   240

HERDSMAN
New arrivals—two young men—have come to our land.
Their boat escaped the dark-blue Clashing Rocks.
What a welcome contribution to our goddess!
Get your holy water ready and your consecrations.   245

IPHIGENIA
Where are they from? What do they look like?

HERDSMAN
Greeks. That's all I know.

IPHIGENIA
You heard no names?

HERDSMAN
One called the other Pylades.

IPHIGENIA
What about his companion?   250

HERDSMAN
Didn't hear, don't know.

IPHIGENIA
Where did you catch them?

HERDSMAN
Down by the edge of the Hostile Sea.

IPHIGENIA
What are herdsmen doing down by the sea?

HERDSMAN
Bathing our oxen in salt water.   255

IPHIGENIA
Go back to the question
where you caught them and how.
This I want to know.
It's been a long time since the goddess' altar ran red with
    Greek blood.°

Well, we were driving our oxen into the water that flows   260
out through the Clashing Rocks.
There was a cleft drilled through by the beat of the sea
where purplefishers shelter.
Here one of us caught sight of two young men.
He came back on tiptoe and said   265
"Look—gods sitting there!"
Another (a pious fellow) lifted his hands to pray:
"Son of sea goddess Leucothea, protector of ships,   270
lord Palaemon, be gracious—
whether those are the twin sons of Zeus there
or some sweet offspring of Nereus
who bore the fifty dancing daughters!"
Then a bold skeptical fellow laughed at the prayers   275
and said it was two shipwrecked sailors
sitting terrified in the cleft—"no doubt they've heard we
    slaughter strangers."
This made sense to most of us.
We decided to take them for the goddess to sacrifice
as per usual.
Meanwhile
one of the strangers came out of the cave. He stood.   280
He tossed his head up and down, howling aloud,
trembling to the tips of his fingers
and staggering in fits.
He cried out like a hunter, "See that one, Pylades?
And there, that snake of hell—look, she's itching to kill me,   285
her horrible snakes are mouthing out at me.
And this one's belching fire and death and thrashing her
    wings,°
she's got a stone shaped like my mother in her arms—
she's going to hurl it!   290
Help, she'll kill me! Where can I run?"

Yet those shapes were not visible.

Only voices of cows and dogs were answering him.°
And we for our part, expecting him to die any minute,
sat crouched in silence.   295
But he drew his sword, leapt among the cattle like a lion
and began laying about him, his blade striking flank and rib,
fantasizing he was driving off the Furies.°
The sea bloomed red with blood.   300
And now
seeing the slaughter of the cows
everyone began to arm himself
and we blew conches to summon the locals
(figuring cowherds were no match for these strong young
     foreigners).   305
We soon had a crowd.
But the stranger let go the pulse of his frenzy
and dropped to the ground.
Foam dripped off his chin.
We all set to work on him, pelting and pounding,
while the other man kept trying to wipe off the foam   310
and shield his friend's body with his cloak,
warding off wounds
and ministering to his friend every way he could.

Now the stranger
all of a sudden sane
jumped up.   315
Saw the tide of foes falling on them° and groaned.
But we did not slack off, kept pitching rocks from this side
     and that.
Then we heard this awful exhortation: 320
"Pylades, we're about to die. Let's die brilliantly!
Draw your sword and follow me!"
At sight of their swords we fled back to the ravines
and as each one fled, others pressed forward   325
bombarding the strangers.
And if these were pressed back

the ones retreating pelted them with stones.
Yet here was the amazing thing:
so many hands throwing—not one hit the victims!
Anyway, in the end, however unheroically, we won the day.   330
Surrounded them and knocked° the swords from their hands
    with rocks.
They sank to their knees exhausted.
We brought them to our king,
who took one look and dispatched them here
for you to wash and sacrifice.   335

Lady, these strangers are exactly the sort of victims
you should pray for.
Execute them and Greece will really be paying you back
for your own murder,
paying the price for that slaughter at Aulis.

CHORUS LEADER
Amazing story!—whoever this man is   340
who's come from Hellas to the Hostile Sea.

IPHIGENIA
Okay, off you go.
Bring the strangers back with you
and we'll attend to sacred duties here.

                                    (*Exit Herdsman to the side.*)

O my poor breaking heart,
once you were kind and compassionate to strangers;   345
you always spared them a kindred tear when they were
    Greeks.
But dreams have ensavaged me.
Whoever you are, you'll find me ill-disposed.   350
This is the truth, it's clear to me, ladies:
our own bad luck does not make us benevolent
toward those who are worse off.
And the thing is,
no breeze of Zeus has ever come here,

no ship brought Helen through the Clashing Rocks   355
with her Menelaus
to pay back what they did to me—
they murdered me!—
to make an Aulis here for that Aulis there
where the Danaans laid their hands on me
as if I were a sacrificial calf
and my own father was the sacrificing priest!   360
I cannot forget those evils!
How many times did I fling my hands at his face crying,
"Father, you marry me to degradation!
While you're killing me here   365
my mother and her women in Argos
are singing wedding songs!
Our house fills with music of pipes
as I die at your hands!
Achilles, it seems, was Hades' son, not Peleus'—
you gave me him as a husband   370
and steered me into a wedding of blood.
It was just a filthy trick!"

And I did not lift my little brother in my arms—
who now is dead!
I did not kiss my sister; no, I
kept my face in veils for I was blushing—
I believed I was going to Peleus' house   375
and put off many an embrace till later,
thinking I'd come back to Argos again.
Poor Orestes—
if you are dead, what a fine patrimony you forfeit!
As for the sophistry of the goddess, I condemn it.   380
She who drives from her altar
anyone who touches blood or childbirth or corpses,
who calls them polluted,
this same goddess revels in human sacrifice!
Impossible the wife of Zeus is mother to such folly!   385

Nor do I credit that story of Tantalus' banquet—
how the gods happily digested a meal of his son.
The people here are murderous themselves,
this is my opinion,
so they ascribe base behavior to their deity.   390
No god is evil, I do not believe it.

CHORUS [*singing*]

STROPHE A

Deep deep blue roads of ocean
where the gadfly out of Argos
crossed the Hostile Sea°   395
from Asia to Europe,
who are these men who left behind the clear Eurotas
green with reeds   400
or the holy streams of Dirce
to come to this implacable country
where the altars and temples of Zeus' daughter   405
are doused with human blood?

ANTISTROPHE A

Did they sail to the double beat of pinewood oars
with ocean billows beneath them°
and an ocean breeze at their back   410
all for greed, for riches to bring home?
Don't fall in love with hope—it can be insatiable.°   415
Men lug rich cargo with them
as they roam strange cities and seas,
all suffering the same delusion.
Some people understand measure;   420
others can't think straight about wealth.

STROPHE B

How did they pass the Clashing Rocks
or the restless shores of Phineus
or the sea-swept coast of Amphitrite   425
where the fifty daughters of Nereus° dance in a circle and sing?
How did they go

racing the waves
with swelling sail
and hissing oar,   430
under southerly breeze
or western wind,
to the land where birds throng the White Shore   435
and Achilles
has his fair running ground
by the edge of the Hostile Sea?

ANTISTROPHE B

I pray along with my lady's prayers
that Helen might leave Troy and come here   440
to die at my lady's hands
with her throat cut   445
and a circle of bloody dew on her hair.
Helen ought to pay!
And how glad I would be
to hear some Greek traveler say
my miserable slavery is at an end.   450
Even in dreams°
how I long to go to my homeland
and share in the happiness there.   455

(Enter Orestes and Pylades from the side escorted by Taurian guards.)

[chanting]
But look, here come the two of them with their hands tied,
fresh victims for the goddess.
That herdsman wasn't lying.
Silence, women.
Choice Greek offerings are at hand.   460
Lady, if you are pleased with these civic rituals,
accept the sacrifice
which our own law calls unholy.   465

IPHIGENIA
So be it.

First I must take care that all arrangements for the goddess
    are correct.
Untie the strangers' hands.
They are sacred and should not be bound.
Now go in and prepare what is needed and proper for our
    task.   470

(Exit the Taurian guards into the temple.)

Ah pity.
Who is the mother who bore you,
the father, the sister—have you a sister?
Robbed of two young men like you
she will be brotherless now.   475
Who can know if his luck will lead in this direction?
Gods' plans are all invisible,
no one knows anything clear.
And luck seduces us sideways to stupidity.

Where did you come from, you poor strangers?
Surely you sailed a long way to get here.   480
And you'll stay a long time underground,
far from home.

ORESTES

Why do you lament these things and vex yourself
over troubles of ours—woman, whoever you are?
It doesn't make sense to me that someone bent on killing
wants to cancel the dread of death with pity.   485
Nor for a man near death with no hope of escape
to pity himself:
he makes one evil into two—
shows himself foolish and dies anyhow.
Let luck go its way.
Sing no dirges for us.   490
We know about the sacrifices here; we understand this.

IPHIGENIA

My first question is, which of you is Pylades?

ORESTES

If it please you, this man is Pylades.

IPHIGENIA

From what city of Greece?   495

ORESTES

What good will it do you to know this, woman?

IPHIGENIA

Are you two brothers, from one mother?

ORESTES

Brothers in love. We are not related.

IPHIGENIA

What sort of name did your father give you?

ORESTES

By rights I should be called Unlucky.   500

IPHIGENIA

Tell that to Fortune, it wasn't my question.

ORESTES

My body, not my name, is what you plan to sacrifice.

IPHIGENIA

Why begrudge this? You think you're so important?

ORESTES

If I die nameless I am spared mockery.

IPHIGENIA

You won't tell me your city either?   505

ORESTES

How will it profit me? I'm about to die.

IPHIGENIA

Then what prevents you granting it as a favor?

ORESTES

Glorious Argos is the home I claim.

IPHIGENIA

By the gods! Stranger, were you really born there?

ORESTES

In Mycenae, once a splendid city.   510

IPHIGENIA

You are surely welcome here if you've come from Argos.°   515

ORESTES

Not by my reckoning! Maybe yours.   516

IPHIGENIA

Did you leave your home as an exile, or why?   511

ORESTES

A kind of exile. Willing and unwilling at once.

IPHIGENIA

Will you tell me something I want to know?

ORESTES

Well, it might distract me from my problems.   514

IPHIGENIA

You've heard of Troy, whose fame is everywhere?   517

ORESTES

How I wish I never had, even in dreams!

IPHIGENIA

They say it is gone, wiped out by war.

ORESTES

That is the case, no idle rumor.   520

IPHIGENIA

And Helen's gone home to Menelaus' house?

ORESTES

She has. And her going brought harm to one of mine.

IPHIGENIA

Where is she now? She owes a debt to me as well.

ORESTES

She lives in Sparta with her former husband.

IPHIGENIA

O object of hatred—for the Greeks, not just me!   525

ORESTES

Yes, I've felt the effect of her marriages too.

IPHIGENIA

And the homecoming of the Achaeans was as reported?

ORESTES

Your questions certainly encompass everything!

IPHIGENIA

I want to make the most of you before you die.

ORESTES

Ask away then, I'll answer your pleasure.   530

IPHIGENIA

Did a prophet named Calchas come back from Troy?

ORESTES

He's dead according to the story at Mycenae.

IPHIGENIA

Excellent! What of Laertes' son, Odysseus?

ORESTES

Not reached home yet, but he lives, they say.

IPHIGENIA

May he perish and never reach home!   535

ORESTES

Don't bother cursing him: his whole life has gone wrong.

IPHIGENIA

And Achilles is alive?

ORESTES

No he is not. A futile marriage he made at Aulis.

IPHIGENIA

A travesty of marriage, so people say who suffered it.

ORESTES

Who are you? Your questions about Greece are strangely apt.   540

IPHIGENIA

I came from there. Was lost as a child.

ORESTES

Naturally you long for news of it, woman.

IPHIGENIA

And what of the general, the one they called "blessedly
    happy"?

ORESTES

I'm not aware of one I'd call "blessedly happy."

IPHIGENIA

A son of Atreus, King Agamemnon, was so called.   545

ORESTES

I don't know. Change the subject.

IPHIGENIA

By the gods, no! Answer my question, stranger!

ORESTES

The poor man is dead. And took another with him.

IPHIGENIA

Dead? How? Oh no! Oh no!

ORESTES

Why do you groan? What's he to you?   550

IPHIGENIA

I groan for the great good fortune he once had.

ORESTES

Hideously he perished, murdered by his wife.

IPHIGENIA

Oh there are tears in this—for the killer and the killed!

ORESTES

Stop now. No more questions.

IPHIGENIA

Just this one: is the poor man's wife alive?   555

ORESTES

No, she is not. Her own son killed her.

IPHIGENIA

O house confounded! What did he want?

ORESTES

To avenge his father dead at her hands.

IPHIGENIA

Pity! He did well then, to carry out so righteous a wrong.

ORESTES

Righteous or not, he wins no grace from gods.   560

IPHIGENIA

And Agamemnon left another child at home?

ORESTES

One daughter, Electra.

IPHIGENIA

Is there not some tale of another daughter, sacrificed?

ORESTES

None except she's dead and looks no more upon the daylight.

IPHIGENIA

Pity that girl, pity the father who slew her.   565

ORESTES

Her death: a thankless gift to an evil woman.

IPHIGENIA

And the dead king's son, he lives in Argos?

ORESTES

He lives in misery, nowhere and everywhere.

IPHIGENIA

False dream, farewell, you were nothing after all!

ORESTES

Nor are the so-called wise gods   570
any more reliable than winged dreams.°

CHORUS LEADER

I feel a sudden sorrow! What of my mother and father—   576
are they alive? Dead? Who can say?

IPHIGENIA

Listen:
I've got a plan, beneficial for you, beneficial for me as well.
And things tend to succeed, do they not,
when one plan is pleasing to all.°   580
Would you be willing, if I saved your life,
to take a message to my loved ones at Argos—
a writing tablet inscribed for me by a captive
who took pity on me once?   585
(He didn't blame me for his murder,
but rather the law of the gods.)°
I've had no one to send the letter with till now.   590
But you are not ill-disposed to me, it seems,
and you know Mycenae, you know the people I mean.
So keep your life and go there—you'll win no mean reward—
salvation in return for a little letter.
And this man here, since the city requires it,   595
can be the goddess' victim, apart from you.

ORESTES

Fine plan, strange lady, except one thing.
This man's death would be a terrible weight on me.
I am captain of this ship of catastrophes;
he sails with me as friend to my need.   600
How unjust for me to win favor myself,
to slip out of harm's way and let him die.
So how about this.
Give the letter to him
(he'll take it to Argos, your purpose is served)
and let whoever wants to kill me kill me.   605
It is utterly base to save oneself
by sabotaging one's friends.
This man is my friend and that's that.
No less than myself I want him to look upon the daylight.

IPHIGENIA

O excellent spirit! What nobility you were born from,
what a true friend you are.   610
I wish my one surviving brother were a man such as you—
yes I do have a brother,
though I never see him.
But since it is your wish, we'll send this fellow
off with the letter
and you shall die.   615
A profound desire for this seems to possess you.

ORESTES

Who will sacrifice me and bear the horror?

IPHIGENIA

I have this duty from the goddess.

ORESTES

Not an enviable duty, girl, nor a lucky one.

IPHIGENIA

But necessary and I must honor it.   620

ORESTES

You, a female, kill men with a sword?

IPHIGENIA

No, but I'll sprinkle sacred water around your head.

ORESTES

Who does the actual slaughtering if I may ask?

IPHIGENIA

Inside this temple are men who have that function.

ORESTES

And what sort of grave will receive me?   625

IPHIGENIA

Sacred fire inside then a wide chasm in the rock.

ORESTES

Ah! How I wish my sister's hand could lay me out!

IPHIGENIA

That is a pointless prayer, you poor man, whoever you are.
She lives far from this barbarian country.
But still, since you're Argive   630
I'll not stint from giving you all I can possibly give.
I shall lay much ornament on your grave,
anoint° your body with yellow oil,
and throw on your fire
the flowery brightness of yellow bees.   635

Well, I go. I shall bring you the letter from the temple.
And so you won't hate me—

(To the servants.)

no fetters.
Guard them here unbound.

I wonder if my news will come as a shock at Argos—
whomever I send to—   640

a shock of incredible joy—
to hear that the one they thought dead is alive!

(Exit into the temple.).

CHORUS [singing]   (To Orestes.)
  I cry for you,
  for your end marked out,
  the bloody rain of lustral water.   645

ORESTES [speaking]
  This needs no pity, strangers, be joyful.

CHORUS [singing]   (To Pylades.)
  But you, young man blessed in fortune,
  we honor you, soon to set foot on your native land.

PYLADES [speaking]
  There is nothing blessed about friends going to their death.   650

CHORUS [singing]
  O grim journey!
  O death near at hand!
  What sorrow! My heart hesitates   655
  which to lament.

ORESTES
  Pylades, by the gods, do you have the same feeling as I?

PYLADES
  I can't say.

ORESTES
  Who is this young girl?
  How very Greek her questions   660
  about the troubles at Troy, the Achaean returns,
  wise Calchas and his birds, the name of Achilles!
  What pity she showed when she asked after poor
      Agamemnon,
  his wife, his children.   665

She comes from there, this strange woman, she is Argive by
  birth
or she would not be sending this letter;
she'd not be probing these matters in general
as if she had some share in the fortunes of Argos.

PYLADES

You're a little ahead of me—still, I agree
except for one thing: 670
this royal family's woes are familiar
to any reasonably alert person.
Still I have another worry.

ORESTES

Share it. You'll think better.

PYLADES

It would be shameful for me to go on living
while you do not.
I sailed with you and I must die with you.   675
Coward and criminal they'll call me in Argos
and in the folded hills of Phocis
if I come home alone.
Most men (most men are malicious) will assume
I betrayed you to get home safely.
Or even murdered you,
plotted your death to get your power,
now that your kingship is tottering   680
and I'm married to your sister who stands to inherit it.
I feel both fear and shame.
For me to breathe my last with you is absolutely the right
  thing.
To be killed and set on a pyre with you, yes.   685
I am your friend. I dread the blame.

ORESTES

Don't say that. My hardships are mine to bear.

Where trouble is single I won't make it double.
You say base and shameful—it's the same for me
if I make you share in my suffering and cause your death.   690
In fact for me personally it's no catastrophe,
faring as I do at the hands of gods,
to cease from life.
But you, you're successful and your house is sound,
not sick. Mine is defiled, unlucky.
Now if you live on and get sons from my sister   695
whom I gave you to wife,
my name will survive,
my ancestral house will not vanish childless.

No, you go. Live your life. Keep my father's house.
And when you reach Greece and horse-breeding Argos,   700
by your right hand I lay this charge upon you:
build me a burial mound and set a monument on it.
Have my sister give tears to the tomb and locks of her hair.
Report how I perished by the hand of some Argive woman
at an altar, consecrated to death.   705
Do not forsake my sister ever,
though you see the marriage, the house, desolate.

And now, farewell. You are the dearest friend I found.
You hunted with me, you shared my upbringing,
you bore with my pains and despairs.   710
Prophetic Apollo betrayed me and lied to me.
He used a trick to drive me as far away from Greece as I
     could go
because he was ashamed of his own former prophecies.
I gave myself to him—trusting his words
I murdered my mother. Now I die in turn!   715

PYLADES
Yes, you will have your burial.
And your sister's bed I'll not betray, O my poor comrade,

for I shall hold you a more beloved friend
dead than living.
Still, the oracle of god has not yet destroyed you
though you stand right next to death.   720
And it is the case, you know it is the case,
that extraordinary misfortune
can call forth extraordinary reversals:
all it takes is luck.

(Enter Iphigenia from the temple.)

ORESTES

Silence! The word of Phoebus is no help to me at all.
And here comes the woman from the house.

IPHIGENIA   *(To servants.)*

Go, go in, get everything ready   725
for the men in charge of the sacrifice.

(To Orestes and Pylades.)

Here is the letter, strangers, folded up tight.
And here's what I want in addition:
no man is the same when he's under stress
as when he regains confidence.   730
My fear is, no sooner he quits this land—
the one who takes my news to Argos—
than he consigns the letter to oblivion.

ORESTES

So what do you want?

IPHIGENIA

Let him swear an oath he will carry this letter   735
to my people in Argos, the ones I choose.

ORESTES

And you'll give such an oath in return?

IPHIGENIA

To do or say what?

ORESTES

To let him go alive from this barbarous land.

IPHIGENIA

That sounds fair. How else could he carry the message?   740

ORESTES

And the king will go along with this?

IPHIGENIA

Yes, I'll persuade him. And put the man on board a boat
myself.

ORESTES   *(To Pylades.)*

Go ahead, swear.

                                                (To Iphigenia.)

And you dictate an oath that's properly pious.

IPHIGENIA

Say "I will give this letter to your loved ones."

PYLADES

I will give this letter to your loved ones.   745

IPHIGENIA

And I will send you safe past the dark-blue rocks.

PYLADES

To which god will you swear this oath?

IPHIGENIA

Artemis, in whose house I hold office.

PYLADES

And I by the king of heaven, sublime Zeus.

IPHIGENIA

And if you forsake your oath and do me wrong?   750

PYLADES

May I never reach home. And you, if you do not save me?

IPHIGENIA

May I never set foot in Argos so long as I live.

PYLADES

Oh but listen, here's a point we've overlooked.

IPHIGENIA

Share it.

PYLADES

Grant me this exception: should something happen to the
    ship   755
so the letter is lost in the waves along with the cargo
and I can save only my skin,
the oath is off.

IPHIGENIA

Here's what I'll do (let's maximize our options):
I'll tell you everything written in the folds of the letter.   760
You can repeat it to my loved ones.
That way we're safe. If you get the letter there intact
it can tell its own tale silently.
But if the writing disappears in the sea
you'll save my words by saving yourself.   765

PYLADES

A good plan for both of us.
Tell me who is to receive the letter
and what to say from you.

IPHIGENIA

Give the message to Orestes, son of Agamemnon:
"The one slaughtered at Aulis sends you word—   770

Iphigenia, who is alive
although at Argos they think otherwise."

ORESTES
Where is she? Come back from the dead?

IPHIGENIA   (*To Orestes.*)
You're looking at her.
Now stop interrupting.

                                                             (*To Pylades.*)

Say "Bring me to Argos before I die, brother,
out of this barbarous land!   775
Free me from my official task
of slaughtering strangers for a goddess!"

ORESTES
What shall I say, Pylades? Where in the world are we?

IPHIGENIA
"Or I'll become a curse on your house, Orestes!"
(That name you'll learn from hearing it twice.)

ORESTES°
O gods!

IPHIGENIA
Why are you invoking gods amid my instructions?   780

ORESTES
No reason. Go on. My mind wandered.
I'm on the verge of some miracle—no more questions.

IPHIGENIA
Tell them Artemis rescued me
by putting a deer in my place,
which my father sacrificed
thinking his sharp knife was slicing into me.   785

The goddess settled me in this land.
That is my message
as written in the letter.

PYLADES

Oh these oaths are easy to swear
and what you swore was beautiful too!
I won't take long to fulfill my vow.

(To Orestes.)

Behold, I bring you this letter from your sister,   790
your sister, Orestes, right here.

ORESTES

And I do welcome it!
But I shall lay the writing aside
and take hold of a joy that is not just words!
O dearest beloved sister, I am stunned   795
but I embrace you with my disbelieving arms
in open joy! This news astounds me!

IPHIGENIA°

Stranger, you transgress! It defiles the servant of a goddess
to touch her inviolable robes.

ORESTES

O my sister, born like me from Agamemnon,   800
don't turn away! You're holding the brother you never
    thought to hold again.

IPHIGENIA

You my brother? Stop this talk! Argos is his territory, and
    Nauplia.

ORESTES

Poor woman, that's not where your brother is.   805

IPHIGENIA

But who is your mother—Tyndareus' daughter from Sparta?

ORESTES

Yes, and my father is grandson of Pelops.

IPHIGENIA

What are you saying? Have you any proof?

ORESTES

Yes. Ask me anything about our father's house.

IPHIGENIA

Shouldn't you go first?   810

ORESTES

Yes. First this, I heard it from Electra:
you know there was strife between Atreus and Thyestes?

IPHIGENIA

Yes, some quarrel about a golden lamb.

ORESTES

So you know you wove it into a fine piece of cloth?

IPHIGENIA

Oh dear one, you come very close to my own heart.   815

ORESTES

And you also wove one showing the sun turned back in its
    course?

IPHIGENIA

I did, I wove this too, into a fine, fine cloth.

ORESTES

And the ritual bath you got from your mother at Aulis?

IPHIGENIA

Yes! There was no happy marriage to cancel that memory.

ORESTES

And what about sending your mother locks of your hair?   820

IPHIGENIA

They belonged on my grave, not my body.

ORESTES

    Now I'll give you the proofs I've seen myself:
    that ancient spear in our father's house—
    the one Pelops wielded
    the day he won Hippodameia at Pisa
    and killed Oenomaus—   825
    it's hidden in your old bedroom.

IPHIGENIA [*singing in this interchange with Orestes, who speaks in reply*]

    O most beloved! Nothing else—you are my most beloved!
    Far from our fatherland, far from Argos,°
    but I have you, O my love.   830

ORESTES

    And I have you,
    though you were dead. So people thought.

IPHIGENIA

    Tears and lamentation mixed with joy,
    make your eyes wet, and mine.
    That day I left you, left you behind, just an infant,
    just a babe in the house.   835
    O happiness greater than words!
    O my soul, what can I say?
    These things have gone far beyond amazement,
    beyond language.   840

ORESTES

    From now on I pray we are happy side by side.

IPHIGENIA

    I cannot place the joy I feel, O my friends, O ladies,
    yet I fear it'll take wing and fly from my hands to the sky!
    O Cyclopean hearth, O fatherland,   845
    O dear Mycenae,
    I thank you for his life,

I thank you for his cherishing:
you've raised a light of salvation for our house,
this brother of mine.

ORESTES
We are blest in our birth
but not in our contingencies, O my sister.   850
Ours is no lucky life.

IPHIGENIA
I realized that
the day my poor father laid his sword on my throat.

ORESTES
O poor love, I was not there but I can see it.   855

IPHIGENIA
There was no wedding song, brother,
when I was so treacherously led to the bed of Achilles.
By the altar instead were tears and lamentations.   860
Alas! I say alas, for the ritual waters poured out there.

ORESTES
Alas! I say it too, for the deed my father dared.

IPHIGENIA
He was no father to me.
Still, things do look different now   865
through some godsent stroke of luck.°   867

ORESTES
Pitiful woman, suppose you had murdered your brother!   866

IPHIGENIA
Pitiful indeed, and I did have it in me to do that!
Dread things I dared, dread things, brother.   870
You barely escaped an unholy death at my hands.
And how will it end?°   875
What chance will arise?

What means will I find to send you away
from violent death in a foreign land
to our home in Argos
before the bloody sword descends on you?   880
O my soul, this is your task: find the way.
Should it be on land, not by sea but on foot?   885
But death is nearby in the form of savage tribes
and impassable roads.
Yet surely that narrow passage through the dark-blue rocks
makes a long journey.   890
Ah, I feel desperate.
What god or mortal or miracle°   895
will find a way where there is no way
and show two lone offspring of Atreus
their exit from evils?

CHORUS LEADER

This is all quite astounding, beyond words—   900
and I saw it with my own eyes!

PYLADES

When loved ones meet, Orestes, it's natural for them
to fall into one another's arms
but now you must leave off emotion and confront the issue:
how shall we win the glorious name of salvation   905
and escape this barbaric land?
It's the mark of a wise man to accept his luck for what it is,°
seize the moment, maximize his happiness.

ORESTES

Well said. And I think we have luck on our side here.
If someone acts resolute, the divine force is more effective
    too.   910

IPHIGENIA

You'll not restrain or silence me until I learn
what fate befell Electra.
This matters a great deal to me.°

ORESTES

She is happily married to Pylades here.   915

IPHIGENIA

And where is he from? Whose son is he?

ORESTES

Strophius of Phocis is his father.

IPHIGENIA

So he's born of a daughter of Atreus—he is my kinsman?

ORESTES

Yes, cousin to you and sole true friend to me.

IPHIGENIA

He was not yet born when my father killed me?   920

ORESTES

No, Strophius was childless a long time.

IPHIGENIA

I greet you, husband of my sister.

ORESTES

And my savior too, not just our kinsman.

IPHIGENIA

But how did you nerve yourself for those horrific deeds
    against our mother?

ORESTES

Let's not talk of it. I was avenging my father.   925

IPHIGENIA

What cause had she to kill her husband?

ORESTES

Let our mother be! It's an evil thing for you to hear.

IPHIGENIA

I am silent. But does Argos look to you now as its leader?

ORESTES

Menelaus rules there. I am exiled from my land.

IPHIGENIA

Surely our uncle did not take advantage of our faltering
house?°   930

ORESTES

No, fear of the Furies drove me away.   931

IPHIGENIA

I understand: the goddesses haunted you for our mother's
sake.   934

ORESTES

To force their bloody bit onto my mouth.   935

IPHIGENIA

Your fit of madness on the shore—was that their doing?   932

ORESTES

Not the first time I've been a spectacle of suffering.   933

IPHIGENIA

But why did you make your way here?   936

ORESTES

On orders from Phoebus.

IPHIGENIA

To do what? Are you permitted to say?

ORESTES

Yes, I can say. Here's how my troubles began:
after I undertook those dread deeds against our mother,
which I pass over in silence,   940
I was driven into exile with the Furies at my heels,
first Delphi,
then Athens, where Apollo sent me°
to render justice to the goddesses whose names we do not
name.

For there is a holy court there established once by Zeus   945
to cleanse Ares' hands of blood pollution.
At first when I arrived
none of my guest-friends was willing to receive me,
a man despised by gods as I am.
But some felt ashamed and gave me a table off by myself
although under the same roof.   950
They addressed no word to me so that
I might enjoy my food and drink apart from them.
Each filled his own jug with equal measure of wine
and took his pleasure.
Pretending not to notice, I challenged no one,   955
suffering in silence
and groaning deep in myself that I was a mother-killer.
(I hear the Athenians made a ritual of my misfortune
and still keep the custom of the Three-Quart Jug.)   960

Then I came to the Hill of Ares and stood trial,
I on one platform, the eldest Fury on the other.
We each said our piece about my mother's murder
and Phoebus saved me with his testimony.   965
Athena counted out the votes: half for me.
I left my own murder trial a victor.
So all the Furies who acceded to the judgment
settled in a holy shrine right near the court.
But the Furies who dissented from the law   970
began to drive me in an endless restless chase
until I came again to Phoebus' holy ground
and laid myself before his sanctuary.
I was starving myself
and I swore I would cut my life off and die there on the spot
if Phoebus did not save me—he had ruined me!   975
Then Phoebus shrieked out from his golden tripod
and sent me here to get the statue that fell from the sky.
I am to set it up in Athens.
Come,

help me accomplish the salvation set out for us.
If we can seize the statue of the goddess
my mad fits will end
and I'll sail you back to Mycenae on our well-oared boat.   980
O dearest beloved, O dear sister's head,
save your father's house, save me!
All is lost for me,
all is lost for the race of Pelops,   985
unless we get our hands on that heaven-dropped statue.

CHORUS LEADER
Some dread wrath of a god has boiled up
against the seed of Tantalus and drives it on through woes.

IPHIGENIA
Since before you came here, brother, I've had an intense
    desire
to be in Argos and set my eyes on you.   990
I want what you want: to release you from troubles
and restore our ailing ancestral home—
for I've no anger left for my killer.
That way I could withdraw my hand from your slaughter
and save our house.
But how to elude the goddess   995
and also the king (when he finds that empty base robbed of
    its statue)
this gives me pause.
How shall I escape death? What story can I come up with?
On the other hand, if our plan works,
you'll take the statue and me on board your fine ship   1000
and the risk dissolves.
Apart from this, I perish,
though you may accomplish your task and get away home.
Well, I do not shrink. Not even if I die to save you.
Because you know, when a man is lost from home   1005
they long for him. But a woman doesn't signify.

ORESTES

  I will not be the murderer of you as well as my mother!
  Her blood is enough. I'm your partner—I want
  to share life and death with you equally.
  I shall bring you home, provided I get there,   1010
  or stay here and die by your side.
  But listen—I wonder, if this were displeasing to Artemis
  why would Loxias give me an oracle
  to take her statue away to Athena's city
  and look upon your face?   1015
  On that calculation, I'm hopeful of achieving our return.

IPHIGENIA

  Yes, how can we both avoid death and get what we want?
  This is the weak point in our homecoming plan,
  though the will is there.

ORESTES

  Could we kill the king?   1020

IPHIGENIA

  Horrific suggestion, for strangers to murder their host.

ORESTES

  But if it will save you and me, worth risking.

IPHIGENIA

  I couldn't do it, but I admire your energy.

ORESTES

  What if you hid me in the temple here?

IPHIGENIA

  Thinking to escape under cover of darkness?   1025

ORESTES

  Yes—night belongs to thieves, daylight to truth.

IPHIGENIA

  There are guards in the temple, we could not elude them.

ORESTES

Oh I give up, we're ruined. What way out is there?

IPHIGENIA

I think I have a new idea.

ORESTES

What? Share it, teach me.   1030

IPHIGENIA

I'll turn your troubles to use in a cunning way.

ORESTES

Women are awfully good at scheming.

IPHIGENIA

I'll declare you came from Argos a murderer of your mother.

ORESTES

Use my misery, if it profits you.

IPHIGENIA

We'll say it isn't permitted to sacrifice you to the goddess.   1035

ORESTES

On what grounds? Or can I guess?

IPHIGENIA

On the grounds you're impure. I'll be keeping the sacrifice
holy.

ORESTES

So how is this better for capturing the statue?

IPHIGENIA

I shall propose to purify you in seawater.

ORESTES

But the statue we need is still in the temple.   1040

IPHIGENIA

And to wash that too. Because you touched it, I'll say.

ORESTES

Where will you go on the sea's wet shore?

IPHIGENIA

To where your ship is moored by its flaxen ropes.

ORESTES

Will you or someone else bring the statue in your hands?

IPHIGENIA

I myself. To touch it is holy for me alone.   1045

ORESTES

And Pylades here, what task will he have?

IPHIGENIA

He'll be said to share the same pollution as you.

ORESTES

You'll do this in secret from the king or not?

IPHIGENIA

I'll win him with words—no way to prevent him noticing.   1049
So you must take care, take very great care, of everything else.   1051

ORESTES

Well, our fine-oared ship is standing ready.°   1050

IPHIGENIA

And one last thing: these women must join in our deception.°   1052

ORESTES

Exhort them, then; find convincing arguments.
A woman has the power to stir pity.
And everything else might just work out perfectly!   1055

IPHIGENIA   (To the Chorus.)

Dearest friends, I look to you.
My fate is in your hands, whether it turn out well
or come to naught with me bereft of my homeland,
my beloved brother, my own dear sister.

Let this be the substance of my appeal: 1060
we are women, as a species devoted to one another,
staunch in defending our common interests.
Keep silence for us and support our attempt to escape.
A loyal tongue is a fine thing.
Look how one turn of fate encircles the three of us   1065
joined in love—to reach home or die.
And besides, if I survive you'll share my good luck,
I'll get you back safe to Greece. Come, I entreat you,
and you, by your right hand, your dear cheek,   1070
your loved ones at home,
by your mother, your father, your child if you have one°—
what do you say? Who says yes, who says no?
Speak out:
if you reject me I perish and my poor brother too.

CHORUS LEADER

Take heart, dear lady. Do but save yourself.   1075
All is silence on my side, as you request,
let great Zeus be witness!

IPHIGENIA

Bless your words and bless your fortunes!

(To Orestes and Pylades.)

Your task now is to enter the temple.
The king will be here any minute   1080
to investigate whether the strangers' sacrifice is done.
O goddess who saved me in the folds of Aulis
from a terrible murdering father's hand,
save me now too along with these men—
or else by your fault is the word of Loxias   1085
discredited among mortals.
Be gracious, depart this barbarous land,
go to Athens.
It is not right for you to dwell here
when you could have a city blessed and happy.

(Exit Iphigenia, Orestes, and Pylades into the temple.)

CHORUS [*singing*]

STROPHE A

Halcyon bird who
all along the rocky sea ridges   1090
sings that song of sorrow
understood by those who know
you always mourn your husband,
how like you I am!—
in my lament
a bird without wings,   1095
longing for Greek marketplaces,
for Artemis goddess of childbirth
who dwells on the Cynthian hill,
for the delicate palm
and the flourishing bay   1100
and the sacred silver olive shoot
so dear to Leto in her travail,
for the lake of circling waters
where a melodious swan
pays service to the Muses.   1105

ANTISTROPHE A

O streams of tears
that fell down my cheeks
the day the towers were toppled,
the day I was shipped off
by enemy oar and enemy spear.   1110
I was trafficked for gold
and got a barbarian home.
Here I serve the girl
who serves deer-killer Artemis—
Agamemnon's daughter,   1115
at an altar where no sheep die.
And I envy the man whose life is solid misery—
amid necessity

he does not grow exhausted
because he lives with it every day.
But happiness keeps shifting. 1120
To fall into evils after good fortune
makes a heavy life for a mortal.

STROPHE B

Now you, lady—an Argive ship
will carry you home
and the waxbound reed of mountain Pan 1125
will call out to the beat of the oars
while prophetic Apollo
singing along with his seven-stringed lyre
brings you safe
to the bright shore of Athens. 1130
But I,°
I will be left behind here
when you go your way on dashing oars
and the sails 1135
of your swift-running ship
are spread to the air.

ANTISTROPHE B

If only I could travel those blazing roads
that fiery Helios travels,
then right above my own chambers at home 1140
I would stop
my wings in midair.
If only I could take my place in the dances°
where once as a girl at fancy weddings 1145
I made my feet whirl
alongside my girlfriends—
we were rivals in grace,
in delicate ornaments
and eager to win the contest.
I decked myself in robes of rich design 1150
and let my hair hang down to shadow my cheeks.

(Enter Thoas from the side.)

THOAS

Where is the woman who keeps these gates,
the Greek? Has she consecrated the strangers already?
Are their bodies ablaze inside the shrine?   1155

(Enter Iphigenia from the temple bearing a statue.)

CHORUS

Here she is, king, she will answer you plainly.

THOAS

Ho there! daughter of Agamemnon!
Why are you hoisting this statue of the goddess off its base?

IPHIGENIA

Stop right there in the doorway, king.

THOAS

Is there something unusual happening in the temple,
Iphigenia?   1160

IPHIGENIA

I spit that away (a word to keep things holy).

THOAS

What are you hinting? Speak out plainly.

IPHIGENIA

The victims you've caught for me are not pure, king.

THOAS

What evidence do you have—or is this your own notion?

IPHIGENIA

The goddess' image turned its back.   1165

THOAS

All on its own or did an earthquake turn it?

IPHIGENIA

All on its own. It closed its own eyes too.

THOAS

For what reason? The pollution of the strangers?

IPHIGENIA

Exactly, yes. Dread deeds were done by them.

THOAS

They murdered some barbarian on the shore?   1170

IPHIGENIA

They were carrying bloodstains from home when they came
here.

THOAS

What bloodstains? I'm very curious.

IPHIGENIA

They cut down their mother with a common sword.

THOAS

Apollo! Not even a barbarian would dare that.

IPHIGENIA

They were pursued all through Greece.   1175

THOAS

So that's why you're bringing the statue out?

IPHIGENIA

Yes, out to the holy open air, away from bloodstains.

THOAS

And how did you discover the strangers' pollution?

IPHIGENIA

I interrogated them when the statue turned around.

THOAS

How perceptive! Greece raised you to be clever.   1180

IPHIGENIA

Besides, they set out a sweet bait for me.

THOAS

Tried to charm you with some news from Argos?

IPHIGENIA

That my only brother, Orestes, is faring well.

THOAS

So you would spare them, I guess, in joy at their news.

IPHIGENIA

And that my father is alive and prospering too.   1185

THOAS

Naturally you remained loyal to the goddess.

IPHIGENIA

Oh yes, I hate Greece utterly. Greece ruined me!

THOAS

Then what should we do about the strangers, tell me.

IPHIGENIA

We must honor the existing law.

THOAS

But aren't your lustrations and sword already at work?   1190

IPHIGENIA

I want to cleanse them first with purifying rituals.

THOAS

In fresh-flowing streams or water of the sea?

IPHIGENIA

The sea washes away all human evil.

THOAS

Yes, they'll be purer victims for your goddess surely.

IPHIGENIA

And that might improve my lot too.   1195

THOAS

Doesn't the sea wash up right here by the temple?

IPHIGENIA

We need a deserted spot—we have other tasks to do.

THOAS

Take them wherever you want. I've no desire to see forbidden
things.

IPHIGENIA

I must purify the goddess' statue as well.

THOAS

Yes you must, if the matricides' pollution touched her.   1200

IPHIGENIA

Why else would I have lifted her from her pedestal?

THOAS

Your piety and forethought are impeccable.

IPHIGENIA

Do you know what I'd like you to do?

THOAS

                                        Tell me.

IPHIGENIA

Tie the strangers up.

THOAS

                                But where could they escape to?

IPHIGENIA

You can't trust anything Greek.

THOAS

                                Servants, fetch ropes.   1205

IPHIGENIA

Let them bring the strangers out here . . .

THOAS

So be it.

IPHIGENIA

. . . Covering their heads with robes.

THOAS

To keep off the gaze of the sun.

IPHIGENIA

Send some of your servants with me.

THOAS

These will attend you.

IPHIGENIA

And send someone to announce to the city . . .

THOAS

What?

IPHIGENIA

. . . that they should all stay indoors.

THOAS

To avoid contact with blood?   1210

IPHIGENIA

Yes, such things do pollute.

THOAS   *(To servant.)*

You, go, make the announcement . . .

IPHIGENIA

. . . that no one come into their sight.

THOAS

How well you care for our city!

IPHIGENIA
And for the friends I have to protect.

THOAS
                                   You mean me!

IPHIGENIA°

THOAS
                    No wonder our whole community admires you.

IPHIGENIA
You yourself stay here before the temple and . . .

THOAS
                                   What shall I do?   1215

IPHIGENIA
. . . cleanse the chamber of the goddess with sulfur.

THOAS
                                   So it's pure for your return.

IPHIGENIA
And when the strangers emerge . . .

THOAS
                                   What should I do?

IPHIGENIA
. . . pull your robe in front of your eyes.

THOAS
                                   So as not to look on a guilty man.°

IPHIGENIA
And if I seem to take too long . . .

THOAS
                                   What limit do I set for this?

IPHIGENIA
. . . don't be surprised.

THOAS

Take your time, do the work
of the goddess properly.   1220

IPHIGENIA
May this purification go according to plan!

THOAS

I second this prayer!

(Enter Orestes and Pylades from the
temple escorted by Taurian guards.)

IPHIGENIA
Here come the strangers now out from the temple.
I see ornaments for the goddess and newborn lambs too—
I shall wash blood with blood to get rid of the defilement—
and blaze of torches and all the other purifications
I ordered for the men and the goddess.   1225
I call upon you citizens to keep your distance from this
    pollution—
anyone who keeps his hands pure as doorkeeper of a temple,
anyone about to enter a marriage,
anyone heavy with child:
keep back, step away, lest this uncleanness fall upon you.
O virgin queen, child of Zeus and Leto,   1230
if I succeed in washing the blood from these men
and performing the requisite sacrifice,
your dwelling will be purified
and we shall prosper.
As for the rest,
I do not say it but I make a sign
to the gods who know more
and to you, goddess.

(Exit Iphigenia, Orestes, and Pylades to the side,
escorted. Exit Thoas into the temple.)

CHORUS [singing]

STROPHE

A fine son is Leto's:
she bore him in the fruitful fields of Delos   1235
a god with golden hair.
He is a master of the lyre and loves
to sight an arrow straight along the bow.
She left the place of her travail and carried her child
from the sheer sea cliffs   1240
to the mother of rushing waters
who dances for Dionysus
on top of Mount Parnassus
where a wine-dark speckle-backed snake,   1245
monster of earth,
glittered from the shade of a laurel tree,
guarding the oracle.°
You were still an infant
bouncing in your mother's arms,   1250
O Phoebus,
when you killed it
and mounted your holy oracle:
now you sit on the golden tripod,
in the place that tells no lies,
dispensing to mortals god-spoken oracles
from your sanctuary   1255
in the middle room of the world
beside Castalia's streams.

ANTISTROPHE

But when he had removed Themis, child of Gaia,°   1260
from her holy oracle,
Earth concocted dream phantoms of night
who revealed things to the cities of men—
how it all began, what came next, the future—   1265
as they slept in their beds wrapped in dark.
So Gaia, jealous for her daughter,

robbed Phoebus of his oracular office.
He went straight to Olympus
on his swift feet, 1270
wrapped his child hands around Zeus' throne
and begged
that the earth goddess' anger be banished
from his Pythian home.
Zeus laughed
to see his son so quick and greedy
for solid gold oblations. 1275
With a shake of his head he stopped the night voices—
stole from mortals those truths that take shape in the night—
gave back his honors to Loxias 1280
and upon those mortals
who throng his throne
he bestowed
trust
in the singing of the god's word.

(Enter Messenger from the side.)

MESSENGER

O temple guards and keepers of the altars,
where is Thoas, king of this land, to be found? 1285
Throw open these bolted doors and call him out.

CHORUS LEADER

Why, if I may ask?

MESSENGER

The two young men are clean gone.
By the schemes of Agamemnon's daughter 1290
they're fleeing this land and taking
the holy image on board their Greek ship.

CHORUS LEADER

That's incredible. But the king you want is not here,
he rushed out of the temple.

MESSENGER

Where to? He needs to know what's happening.   1295

CHORUS LEADER

No idea. Run after him, find him
and tell him your news.

MESSENGER

See how treacherous is the female species!
You too have some share in these goings-on, don't you?

CHORUS LEADER

You're mad. What would escaping foreigners have to do
    with us?   1300
And shouldn't you be hastening off to the palace gates?

MESSENGER

Not until an interpreter tells me
whether the king is inside or not.
Hey, you inside, undo these bolts!
And tell your master I'm here at the door   1305
with a boatload of bad news.

                          (Enter Thoas from the temple.)

THOAS

Who's making this racket at the house of the goddess,
banging doors, interrupting us inside?

MESSENGER

These women lied to me,° kept trying to drive me away,
said you were out. But you were here all the time!   1310

THOAS

Why? What did they think to gain?

MESSENGER

I'll explain that later. Listen to what's happening right now.
The young girl who was in charge of the altar here, Iphigenia,
has fled the land along with the strangers   1315
and the holy statue. The purification was a trick.

THOAS

What do you mean? What lucky breeze did she catch?

MESSENGER

She is saving Orestes. Surprise for you!

THOAS

Who? You mean the boy who is son of Tyndareus' daughter?

MESSENGER

Yes, and the one who'd been dedicated by the goddess for this
    altar.   1320

THOAS

That's amazing! What more can I say?

MESSENGER

Don't fuss about it, just hear me out:
when you've thoroughly listened and pondered,
plan a way to track those foreigners down.

THOAS

You're right, go ahead. They have no short voyage   1325
ahead of them if they think to escape my spear.

MESSENGER

Well, when we came to the shore of the sea
where Orestes' ship was secretly anchored,
holding on to those strangers' ropes as you bid us,
Agamemnon's daughter signaled us to stand back   1330
saying she was kindling forbidden fire
and performing special purificatory rites.
Then she took their ropes in her own hands
and walked behind them.
Now this was suspicious
but your servants went along with it, my lord.   1335
After a while, to give the impression she was doing
    something,
she let out an ululation and started chanting

barbarian songs, as if she were
some kind of priest cleansing blood pollution.

And when we'd been sitting a long time on the ground
it struck us that once they were set free   1340
the strangers might kill her and make their escape.
We sat in silence, afraid to look at things forbidden.
But finally the same conclusion came to us all,
to go where they were, forbidden or not.
There we saw the Greek ship   1345
fitted with oars that spread out like wings
and fifty sailors holding their oars on the pins
and the young men—loose from their bonds—
standing on the stern.
Some sailors were holding the bow with poles,   1350
some were fastening the anchor to its supports,
others hastened to lower ladders from the stern
into the sea for the foreign woman.

Well, we lost restraint now that we'd seen her treachery.
Laying hold of the foreign woman and the stern ropes   1355
we began pulling the steering oars out of their sockets.
Words went back and forth:
"What's your explanation—making off from our land
with statues and priestesses?
Who are you, whose son are you, trafficking this woman
    away?"   1360
The other replied:
"I am Orestes, for your information,
brother of this woman, son of Agamemnon.
And the woman I'm transporting is my own sister, lost from
    home."
Still we held on to her,
trying to force her to come along with us to you.   1365
That's how I got these terrible knocks on the jaw!
They had no iron to hand, nor had we,
but fists were pummeling

and kicks were landing from both young men at once
onto our ribs and livers—   1370
the pain was intense, our limbs grew exhausted.
Covered in awful marks we fled to the cliff,
bloody and wounded on heads and faces.
Then taking a stand on the hill we fought more cautiously   1375
and pelted with rocks.
But archers stationed on the ship's stern
were hindering us with arrows and keeping us back.
Meanwhile
a monstrous wave had run the ship aground
and the girl° was afraid to wet her foot   1380
so Orestes took her on his left shoulder,
stepped into the sea and leapt onto the ladder,
setting his sister down on the well-benched ship
along with that thing that fell from the sky—
the image of Zeus' daughter.
And from midship there came a shout: 1385
"You band of sailors from the land of Greece,
take your oars, make the sea white with foam.
We have the prize for which we sailed through
the hostile passage of the Clashing Rocks."

They roared out a glad shout   1390
and struck the salt sea. And so long as the ship
was within the harbor it kept advancing
but as it crossed the mouth
it went under
the deluge of a violent wave.
For a terrible wind came up suddenly
and was thrusting the ship backward.
They persevered, kicking against the wave,   1395
but a back-rushing surf was driving the ship to land.
Then Agamemnon's daughter stood up and prayed:
"O daughter of Leto,
send me, your priestess, safe

back to Greece from this barbarian land
and forgive my thievery.   1400
You surely love your brother, goddess.
Know that I too love my kin."

The sailors seconded the girl's prayer with a paean
and at a command put their bare shoulders to the oars.   1405
But the boat was coming more and more toward the rocks.
Then one of our men leapt into the sea on foot,
another tried to catch the woven ropes,
and I was sent straight here to you
to let you know what's happening over there, king.   1410
Go then, bring bonds and ropes with you.
For unless the rising sea turns quiet again
there is no hope of salvation for these strangers.
Reverend Poseidon, ruler of the ocean and
watcher over Troy, is hostile to Pelops' family.   1415
And now it seems he will deliver Agamemnon's son
into your hands—yours and your citizens'—
along with his guilty sister—she who forgot
the sacrifice at Aulis and betrayed her own goddess.

CHORUS LEADER
    O poor Iphigenia, you will die with your brother
    now you've fallen again into the tyrant's hands.

THOAS
    I address you all, people of this barbarian land.
    Come, throw reins on your horses and race along the shore
    to welcome the wreck of the Greek ship,   1425
    and while some of you hurry to hunt down these impious
        men
    with the help of the goddess,
    others will drag swift vessels into the water
    so we can take them by sea and ride them down on land,
    then throw them off a steep rock   1430
    or skewer their bodies on stakes!

And you women who collaborated in these plots,
I'll punish you later at my leisure.
Right now I'm busy, can't linger.

(Enter Athena above the temple.)

ATHENA

Where oh where are you off to on this hot pursuit, King
    Thoas?   1435
Hear what I, Athena, have to say!
Stop your hunting; don't launch the full flood of your men.
It was fated by Loxias' oracles for Orestes to come here
fleeing the anger of Furies,
to transport his sister back home to Argos   1440
and bring the holy image to my land,
so to find rest from his toils.
This is the word I have for you.
As for Orestes,
whom you expect to catch and kill on the tossing sea,
Poseidon is even now, as a favor to me,
smoothing the waves for his oar to traverse.   1445
Orestes (you do hear my divine voice
though you are not present),
heed my instructions.
Take the image and your sister and go.
When you reach god-built Athens,   1450
there is a place near the far edge of Attica,
close by the hills of Carystus,
a holy place called Halae by my people.
There build a temple and set down the statue.
Call it "Tauric" after the Taurian land
and the ordeals you survived,
roaming up and down Greece goaded by Furies.   1455
People in future will hymn her as Artemis Tauropolus.
And you must establish this custom:
when they celebrate her festival
let them hold a sword at a man's throat and draw blood,   1460

in payment for your sacrifice—so to mark its sanctity
and let the goddess keep her honors.
Now you, Iphigenia,
must continue to hold the keys of this goddess
in the holy meadows of Brauron.
There you will die and be buried
and they will make an offering to you
of finewoven robes left behind in their homes   1465
by women who die in childbirth.
As for these women of Greece—I command you
to send them from this country
as reward for their righteousness.°
I rescued you once already, Orestes,
on the Hill of Ares when I judged the votes equal.   1470
This too shall become customary:
whoever gets equal votes will win his case.
Go then, child of Agamemnon,
bring your sister out of this land.
And you, Thoas, calm your rage.

THOAS

Queen Athena, that man is not in his right mind   1475
who hears gods' words and disobeys.
I harbor no rage against Orestes for departing with the
    image,
nor against his sister.
Is there any good in fighting powerful gods?
Let them go to your land and take the goddess' statue,   1480
let them enshrine it there with all success.
I will also send these women to blessed Greece
as you enjoin me.
And I will no longer raise my spear,
nor my ship's oars,
against the strangers,
since this is your will, goddess.   1485

ATHENA
    I commend you.
    Necessity governs both you and the gods.
    Go, winds, convey the son of Agamemnon to Athens.
    I shall accompany the voyage
    to keep my sister's sacred image safe.

                                        (Exit Athena.)

THOAS [*chanting*]
    Go on your way rejoicing in good fortune,°   1490
    blessed by salvation.

CHORUS [*chanting*]
    O holy among immortals and mortals,
    Pallas Athena,
    we will do as you bid.
    Surely delightful and unexpected   1495
    is this utterance I hear.
    O great holy Victory,°
    may you uphold my life
    and not cease to crown me with crowns.

                                        (Exit all.)

ION

Translated by RONALD FREDERICK WILLETTS

ION: INTRODUCTION

The Play: Date and Composition

It is not certain when *Ion* was first produced, but various metrical considerations, the rather experimental way in which Euripides makes use of the three actors, and perhaps also a couple of (rather doubtful) allusions to contemporary events combine to suggest a date of around 413 BCE (though a date as early as 418 or 417 has also been proposed). Presumably Euripides wrote *Ion* for the annual competition at the Great Dionysian Festival in Athens. We do not know what the other three plays were in his tetralogy that year, or how they fared in the competition.

The Myth

Despite the play's title, its central character is really Creusa, the daughter of Erechtheus, legendary early king of Athens. As a teenager, Creusa was raped by the god Apollo. She became pregnant and abandoned the baby boy to death, but he was rescued by the god and brought to his shrine at Delphi, where he was named Ion and, ignorant of his own identity, was raised by the priestess as a temple servant. In the meantime, Creusa has married the foreigner Xuthus in recompense for his military service to Athens, but their marriage has been childless. As the play begins, Xuthus and Creusa have come to Delphi to find out if they will have children (and so that Creusa can learn the fate of her child). Apollo, wishing to help his son by establishing him as eventual ruler in Athens, has his oracle declare to Xuthus that Ion is Xuthus' son. But when Creusa finds out that Xuthus apparently has a son by a different woman while she herself seems fated to remain childless, she decides to murder Ion. Her plot goes awry, and Ion and the Delphians seek vengeance on her. At the last minute, Apollo prompts the Delphian priestess to show Ion the birth tokens that had accompanied him as a baby; Creusa, who had given them to him when she abandoned him, recognizes them, and so mother and son are joyously reconciled with one another and Creusa reveals to Ion that Apollo is his father. But Ion is not yet satisfied: he is about to rush into the temple and question Apollo directly— when suddenly Athena appears and foretells a glorious future for Ion in Athens and for his descendants, the "Ionians," in Europe and Asia.

Euripides' *Ion* is one of the very few surviving Greek tragedies—along with Aeschylus' *Eumenides* and Sophocles' *Oedipus in Colonus*—to be concerned especially with the local legends of Athens. Ion, Creusa, and Xuthus are all important and interconnected figures in Athenian mythology and political ideology of the fifth century, though their exact family relations with one another were reported differently by different sources. They have in common that they belong to an intermediate period after such primeval and rather monstrous figures as Erechtheus, Cecrops, and Erichthonius, and before the members of later royal dynasties, the Erechthids and the Melanthids, who, though doubtless not much more real historically, at least were thought of as being more thoroughly human. In different ways, Creusa (a member of the legitimate royal line who marries a foreigner) and Xuthus (a foreigner who is brought into the dynasty because of his military service to Athens) both help mediate between the autochthony of which the Athenians were so proud and the external elements to which their culture owed so much. In some versions, Ion is the son of Xuthus, but in Euripides' play (perhaps by the playwright's innovation) he is in fact the son of Apollo and only putatively that of Xuthus. His cultural importance to the Athenians is especially that, as the namesake and founder of the Ionian race, he justifies the Athenian claim to preeminence among the Ionians.

For the Athenian spectators of *Ion*, the main characters were surely all familiar, though perhaps rather shadowy. Euripides has invented a play in which these characters are intimately involved with one another in a plot full of sudden surprises and unforeseeable twists on the way to a largely happy ending. Sophocles is known also to have written an *Ion* and a *Creusa*; but these plays have been lost except for a few fragments, and it is unknown whether they presented any of the same mythic material as Euripides' *Ion*, whether they preceded or followed this play, whether there was any influence from the one tragedian on the other—and indeed even whether the two Sophoclean titles refer to one tragedy or to two.

Transmission and Reception

Ion has an exciting plot based upon an abandoned infant, parents without a child and a child without parents, concealment and disclosure, misidentification and recognition. After a series of confusing, astonishing, and emotionally wrenching turns, it ends happily with a joyous mutual recognition. Thus the play points ahead to the plot structures of such New Comedy playwrights as Menander and to the prose romances of later Greek literature.

But if the kind of play *Ion* represents seems to have been successful with later Greek audiences and readers, the same cannot apparently be said about the specific play itself. For this very locally focused story was surely of greatest interest only to the Athenians, and was not likely to remain so popular in later centuries and in other parts of the Greek-speaking world. So the play survived antiquity only by the accident of being among the so-called alphabetic plays (see "Introduction to Euripides," p. 3), and it is transmitted only by a single manuscript (and its copies) and is not accompanied by the ancient commentaries (scholia) that explain various kinds of interpretative difficulties. Further evidence of its limited popularity in antiquity is that not even one papyrus bearing any part of its text has been discovered and that only a few passages are ever quoted by later Greek authors.

In modern times, too, *Ion* has not been as popular as it deserves to be. At the beginning of the nineteenth century, August

Wilhelm von Schlegel wrote a tragedy, *Ion*, based on Euripides' play, which Goethe directed at its premiere in Weimar in 1803. At the end of the century, Leconte de Lisle composed a French verse drama on the subject, *L'Apollonide* ("The Son of Apollo"). In the past century, the play drew the attention of two important English poets: H.D. (Hilda Doolittle), who began a translation of it in 1927; and especially T. S. Eliot, who wrote a remarkable verse drama based on it (*The Confidential Clerk*, 1953). And in 1983-84 the French philosopher Michel Foucault devoted a substantial part of his penultimate set of lectures at the Collège de France, on freedom of speech, to *Ion*.

I◇N

Characters   HERMES
ION, son of Creusa and Apollo
CHORUS (of Creusa's young female attendants)
CREUSA, mother of Ion, and wife of Xuthus
XUTHUS, king of Athens and husband of Creusa
OLD MAN, a servant of Creusa
A SERVANT of Creusa
PRIESTESS of Apollo at Delphi
ATHENA

Scene: In front of the temple of Apollo at Delphi, just before sunrise.

(Enter Hermes.)

HERMES

Atlas, who wears on back of bronze° the ancient
abode of gods in heaven, had a daughter
whose name was Maia, born of a goddess:
she lay with Zeus and bore me, Hermes, servant
of the immortals. I have come here to Delphi   5
where Phoebus sits at earth's midcenter, gives
his prophecies to men, and makes pronouncement
of what is happening now and what will come.

        For in the famous city of the Greeks
called after Pallas of the golden spear,
Phoebus compelled Erechtheus' daughter Creusa   10
to accept his violent embrace—at that site
below Athena's hill whose northern scarp

the Attic lords have named the Long Rocks.
Her father, by the god's own wish, did not
suspect, and so she carried the child in secret.   15
And when the time had come, her son was born,
inside the palace. Then she took the child
to the same cave where she had lain with Phoebus,
and in a wicker cradle there exposed
him to his death. But she maintained a custom   20
begun a long time ago, when Athena placed
beside Erichthonius, son of Earth, two snakes
as guardians, when the daughters of Aglaurus
were given charge of him. And ever since
Erechtheus' descendants have the custom there
of placing by their babies when they raise them
snakes made of beaten gold.

                    So Creusa tied   25
to him whatever girlish ornaments
she had, before she left him to his death.
My brother Phoebus made me this request:
"You know Athena's city well," he said.
"Now will you journey to the earth-born people   30
of glorious Athens? There, inside a cave
a newborn child is hidden. Take the child,
his cradle, and his swaddling clothes and bring
them to my oracle at Delphi, then
set them near the shrine's door. Just so you know,   35
the child is mine. I will arrange the rest."

        I did as Loxias my brother wished,
took up the wicker cradle, brought it here,
setting it on the temple steps, and then
I opened up the basket, so the child
could be seen. Now when the sun began to ride   40
in heaven, a priestess was just entering
the oracular shrine. Her eyes were drawn toward
the helpless child. Astonished that a girl
of Delphi should dare to cast her secret child

before Apollo's temple, she would have taken it   45
outside the sacred precinct, but her pity
expelled the cruel impulse—and the god
helped too, to keep his son within his house.
And so she took the child and reared him,
not knowing who his mother was, or that   50
Apollo was his father, while the child
has never known his parents. His childhood home
has been about the altars where he played
and ate his meals. But when he was fully grown,
the Delphians appointed him their steward,   55
the trusted guardian of Apollo's gold.
And he has lived a holy life until
this day, within the shrine.
                          Creusa, whose son
he is, has married Xuthus. This is how
the marriage occurred. A war arose between
Athens and Chalcodon's people in Euboea;   60
Xuthus as an ally helped to end the strife,
and though he was not a native, but Achaean,
son of Aeolus, son of Zeus, the prize
he won was marriage to Creusa. But
in all these years no children have been born.   65
Desire for children is now bringing them
to Apollo's shrine. Though Apollo seems unaware,
it's he controls their fate and guides them here.
When Xuthus comes before the shrine, the god
will give him his own son, declaring Xuthus   70
the father. Thus the boy shall be received
into his mother's house and made known to her.
And while Apollo's love affair stays secret,
his son will have what is his due. Moreover,
Apollo will bestow on him the name
of Ion, make that name renowned through Greece   75
as founder of cities in Asia.
                             Now, because

I wish to see this young boy's destiny
complete, I shall conceal myself within
these laurel groves. Here is Apollo's son,
who comes out now, with branches of bay, to make
the portals bright before the temple. And I
will be the first of all the gods to call   80
him by his future name of—Ion.

(Exit to the side. Enter Ion from the temple, carrying a bow
and arrows and accompanied by Delphian servants.)

ION [chanting]
Look, now the sun's burning chariot comes
casting his light on the earth.
Banned by his flame, the stars flee
to the sacred darkness of space.   85
The untrodden peaks of Parnassus,
kindling to brightness, receive for mankind
the disk of the day.
              The smoke of unwatered myrrh drifts
to the top of the temple.   90
The Delphian priestess sits on the
sacred tripod chanting to the Greeks
echoes of Apollo's voice.
              You Delphians, attendants of Phoebus,
go down to Castalia's silvery eddies: 95
when you have bathed in its holy dews,
return to the temple.
Let your lips utter no words
of ill omen; may your tongues
be gracious and gentle to those who   100
come to the oracle.

(Exit the attendants to the side.)

       As for myself, mine is the task
I have always done since my childhood.
With these branches of bay and these sacred

garlands I will brighten Apollo's
portals, cleanse the floor with   105
sprinklings of water,
put to flight with my arrows the birds
that foul the offerings.
Since I have neither mother nor father,
I revere the temple of Phoebus   110
that has nursed me.

[singing]

STROPHE

Come, fresh-blooming branch
of lovely laurel,
with which I sweep clean
the precinct below the shrine,   115
sprung from the eternal garden
where the sacred spring sends
a gushing, never failing stream
from the myrtle grove
to water the sacred leaves,   120
leaves I brush over his temple,
all day long serving with my daily task
when the sun's swift wing appears.

O Healer! O Healer!   125
My blessing! My blessing!
O Leto's son!

ANTISTROPHE

Fair, fair is the labor,
O Phoebus, which
I am doing for you,
honoring the prophetic place.   130
I have a glorious task:
to set my hands to serve
not a man but the immortals.
I will never weary

over my pious tasks.   135
I praise him who feeds me, Phoebus
my father—his love deserves the name,
Phoebus, lord of the temple.   140

O Healer! O Healer!
My blessing! My blessing!
O Leto's son!

Now I shall finish my sweeping
with my broom of bay,   145
I shall pour from golden bowls
water risen from the earth,
drawn from the spring
of Castalia.
Myself holy and chaste, I can
sprinkle the lustral water.   150
Always thus may I serve Phoebus,
service without end—
or an end that comes with good luck.

        Look! Look!
Here come the birds already,
leaving their nests on Parnassus.   155
Keep away from the cornices
and the gold-decked abode.
I will strike you too with my arrows,
you herald of Zeus,
though your beak is strong,
surpassing the other birds.   160
Here sails another to the temple steps,
a swan.—Take to another place
your red shining feet.
You may have your music,
but Apollo's lyre will not save you
at all from my bow;   165
turn your wings,

speed on to the lake of Delos.
If you do not obey,
you will scream laments,°
not that clear-toned song.
      Look! Look!   170
What is this other bird here on its way?
Is it going to build in the cornice
a nest of dry twigs for its young?
The twang of my bow will prevent you.
Go, I tell you, and rear
your young in the eddies of Alpheus   175
or the Isthmian grove,
without fouling the offerings
and Apollo's shrine.°
Yet I scruple to kill you
who announce to mankind
the will of the gods.   180
But I will bend to the labors
of my devotion to Phoebus,
never ceasing to honor him
who gives me nurture.

        (Exit Ion into the temple. Enter the Chorus, young girl servants
              of Creusa, from the side. They admire the temple.)

CHORUS°[singing]

                   STROPHE A
Not only in holy Athens after all
are there courts of the gods   185
with fair columns, and homage paid
to Apollo who protects the streets.
Here too on this temple
of Leto's son shows
the bright-eyed beauty of twin façades.

Look, look at this: Zeus's son   190
is killing the Lernaean Hydra

with a golden sickle,
look there, my dear.

Yes—and near him another is raising
on high a flaming torch.   195
Can it be he whose story I hear
as I sit at my weaving,
Iolaus the shield-bearer,
companion of Heracles,
whom he helped to endure his labors?   200

And look at this one
on a horse with wings.
He is killing the mighty three-bodied
fire-breathing monster.

My eyes dart everywhere.   205
See! The battle of the Giants
on the marble walls.

Yes we are looking.

Can you see her, brandishing
her Gorgon shield against Enceladus—?   210
I can see my goddess Pallas Athena.

Oh! The terrible thunderbolt
with fire at each end which Zeus holds
ready to throw.

Yes I see. Raging Mimas
is burnt up in the flames.   215

And Bacchus, the boisterous god,
with unwarlike wand of ivy is killing
another of Earth's giant sons.

(Enter Ion from the temple.)

CHORUS [*singing in this lyric interchange with Ion, who chants in reply*]

You there by the temple,
may we with pale feet   220
pass into this sanctuary°?

ION

You may not, strangers.

CHORUS

Perhaps you would tell me?

ION

Tell me, what do you want?

CHORUS

Is it true that Apollo's temple
really contains the world's center?

ION

Yes, wreathed in garlands, flanked by Gorgons.

CHORUS

That is the story we have heard.   225

ION

If you have offered sacrificial cake
in front of the temple, and you have a question
for Apollo to answer, come to the altar steps.
But do not pass into the inner shrine
unless you have slaughtered a sheep.

CHORUS

I understand.
We are not for transgressing Apollo's law.   230
The outside charms us enough.

ION

Look where you please at what is lawful.

[219]   ION

CHORUS

Our masters have allowed us
to look over this sanctuary of Apollo.

ION

In whose house do you serve?

CHORUS

The dwelling place of Pallas   235
is the house of our masters.
But the person you ask about is here.

(Enter Creusa from the side.)

ION [now speaking]

Whoever you may be, you are noble,°
your looks reveal your character: by looks
nobility is often to be judged.   240
But?—you surprise me—why, your eyes are closed,
that noble face is wet with tears—and now!
when you have seen Apollo's holy temple.
What reason can there be you're so upset?
Where others are glad to see the sanctuary,   245
your eyes are filled with tears.

CREUSA

That you should be surprised about my tears
is not ill-bred. But when I saw this temple,
I measured an old memory again;   250
my mind was elsewhere, although I'm standing here.
        Unhappy women! What things the gods dare! And where
shall we turn for justice when we are being destroyed
by the unjust actions of those who are much stronger?

ION

What is the cause of this strange melancholy?   255

CREUSA

Nothing. Now I have shot my arrow I shall
be silent, and you should not think of it.

ION

    But tell me who you are, your family,
    your fatherland. And say what is your name?

CREUSA

    Creusa is my name, from Erechtheus   260
    I was born, and Athens is my land.

ION

    A famous city and a noble family!
    How fortunate you are!

CREUSA

    Yes, fortunate in that—but nothing else.

ION

    There is a story told—can it be true . . .   265

CREUSA

    But tell me what it is you want to know.

ION

    . . . your father's ancestor sprang from the earth?

CREUSA

    Yes, Erichthonius—but ancestry is no help.

ION

    Athena really took him from the earth?

CREUSA

    Into her virgin arms, though she was not his mother.   270

ION

    And then she gave him, as we see in paintings . . .

CREUSA

    To Cecrops' daughters, to keep without looking at him.

ION

    I have been told they opened up the cradle.

CREUSA

And died for it. The rocks were stained with blood.

ION

Oh. The other story? Is that true or not?   275

CREUSA

Which one is that? I have time to answer.

ION

Well, did your father sacrifice your sisters?

CREUSA

He had the courage. They were killed for Athens.

ION

How was it you were saved, the only one?

CREUSA

I was a baby in my mother's arms.   280

ION

And it's true your father was buried in a chasm?

CREUSA

Yes; the sea god's trident blows destroyed him.

ION

There is a place there which is called Long Rocks?

CREUSA

Oh, why ask that? You've stirred my memory.

ION

Phoebus° with his lightning honors it.   285

CREUSA

Honor? What honor?° I wish I'd never seen it.

ION

Why do you hate a place the god so loves?

CREUSA

No matter. But I know its secret shame.

ION

And what Athenian became your husband?

CREUSA

My husband is no citizen of Athens.   290

ION

Who then? He must have been of noble birth.

CREUSA

Xuthus, the son of Aeolus and Zeus.

ION

A foreigner! How could he marry an Athenian?

CREUSA

A neighboring land of Athens is Euboea.

ION

Which has a sea for boundary, they say.   295

CREUSA

Athens conquered it with the help of Xuthus.

ION

He came as ally? You were his reward?

CREUSA

Dowry of war, the prize won with his spear.

ION

And have you come alone or with your husband?

CREUSA

With him. But he's still at Trophonius' shrine.   300

ION

To see it or consult the oracle?

CREUSA

To ask the same as he will ask of Phoebus.

ION

Is it about your country's crops? Or children?

CREUSA

Though married long ago, we have no children.

ION

No children? You have never had a child?   305

CREUSA

Apollo knows about my childlessness.

ION

Ah! That misfortune cancels all your blessings.

CREUSA

And who are you? Your mother must be happy!

ION

I am what I am called, Apollo's slave.

CREUSA

A city's votive gift or sold by someone?   310

ION

I only know that I am called Apollo's.

CREUSA

So now it is my turn to pity you!

ION

Because my parents are unknown to me.

CREUSA

You live inside the temple? Or at home?

ION

Apollo's home is mine, wherever I sleep.   315

CREUSA

    And did you come here as a child, or youth?

ION

    An infant is what they say who seem to know.

CREUSA

    What Delphian woman was it who suckled you?

ION

    No breast fed me. But she who reared me up . . .

CREUSA

    Yes, who, poor child? Both of us have sorrows!   320

ION

    . . . was Phoebus' prophetess, for me a mother.

CREUSA

    But what gave nurture to you as you grew up?

ION

    The altars and the visitors who came.

CREUSA

    And your unhappy mother! Who was she then?

ION

    Perhaps I was born from an injustice that she suffered.   325

CREUSA

    You are not poor. Your robes are fine enough.

ION

    These robes belong to him, the god I serve.

CREUSA

    But have you never tried to find your parents?

ION

    How can I when I have no clues to guide me?

CREUSA

Ah yes.
Another woman suffered, just as your mother did.   330

ION

Who was she? If she could only share my grief!

CREUSA

On her behalf I came before my husband.

ION

Why did you come? Tell me and I will help.

CREUSA

I need a secret prophecy from Phoebus.

ION

Just tell me. All the rest I'll do for you.   335

CREUSA

Then hear this story. But I am ashamed!

ION

Then you'll get nothing done. Shame's unassertive.

CREUSA

I have a friend who says she lay with Phoebus.

ION

Not Phoebus and a mortal woman! No!

CREUSA

And had a child unknown to her own father.   340

ION

She is ashamed to admit some man's misdeed.

CREUSA

But she says not. Her life has been most wretched.

ION

Why, if it was a god who was her lover?

CREUSA

She put from out the house the child she bore.

ION

Where is the child? Is it still alive?   345

CREUSA

I have come here to ask, for no one knows.

ION

If he is dead now, how then did he die?

CREUSA

Killed by wild beasts, is what she thinks.

ION

What reason could she have for thinking so?

CREUSA

She could not find him when she went again.   350

ION

But were there drops of blood upon the ground?

CREUSA

She says there were not, though her search was careful.

ION

And how long is it since the child was done for?

CREUSA

If he still lived, he would have been your age.

ION

Apollo is unjust. She has my pity.   355

CREUSA

And she has never had another child.

ION

Supposing Phoebus has reared him up in secret?

CREUSA

To keep that pleasure for himself is wrong.

ION

Ah! This misfortune echoes my own grief.

CREUSA

And some unhappy mother misses you?°   360

ION

Do not revive the grief I had forgotten.

CREUSA

I'm sorry. But you'll do as I request?

ION

But do you know where that request is faulty?

CREUSA

What is not faulty for that wretched woman?

ION

Will Phoebus tell the secret he wants to hide?   365

CREUSA

Yes, if his oracles are open to all Greeks.

ION

He feels ashamed. Do not embarrass him.

CREUSA

But the one who suffered from it is in pain!

ION

No one will speak the truth on your behalf.
Convicted of evil inside his own temple,   370
Apollo quite justly would take vengeance on
the one who told you. Think no more of it:
avoid a question which the god himself opposes.
Such foolishness we would commit in trying°
to force reluctant answers from the gods,   375

whether by slaying sheep before the altar
or taking omens from the flight of birds.
The benefits we seek by force against
the gods' will are no use. We only profit
by what they give us of their own free will.   380

CHORUS LEADER

Humans are many, and their woes are many,
the forms of woe diverse. One life of happiness
is seldom to be found in humankind.

CREUSA

Apollo! Then and now unjust to her,
the absent woman whose complaints are here.   385
You did not save the child you should have saved.
A prophet, you have no answer for his mother,
so if he's dead, at least he could be buried,
or, if alive, come to his mother's gaze.
But now that hope must die,° because the god   390
prevents me learning what I wish to know.
          But I can see my noble husband, Xuthus,
arriving from Trophonius' cave. He is
quite near; I beg you, stranger, tell him nothing
of what we have been saying. Or I may   395
be suspect, meddling in these secret matters,
and then this story will not have the end
we have designed. For trouble is very easy
when women deal with men. And since good women
are mixed with bad ones, all of us are hated.
To this misfortune we women are all born.   400

(Enter Xuthus from the side.)

XUTHUS

My greeting first of all is to the god,
and then to you my wife.
                          But can it be
that my delay has caused you some alarm?

[229] ION

CREUSA

No. Your arrival has prevented that.
What oracle did Trophonius give about   405
our hopes of having children?

XUTHUS

He was unwilling to anticipate
Apollo's answer. But he has told me this,
that neither you nor I shall go from here
without a child.

CREUSA

O holy mother of Apollo, may   410
our journey here end well, our dealings with
your son have a happier outcome than before!

XUTHUS

So it will be! But who speaks here for Phoebus?

ION

Sir, that is my duty here outside the temple—
inside are others, near the tripod, nobles   415
of Delphi, who have been chosen by lot.

XUTHUS

Ah! Good. I now know all I need to know,
and shall go in. They say the victim, which
is offered on behalf of visitors, has
already fallen before the altar. Omens   420
today are good, and I would like to have
my answer from the oracle. Will you,
Creusa, with laurel branches in your hand,
go round the altars praying to the gods
that I may bring an oracle with promise
of children for us from Apollo's house.

(Exit Xuthus into the temple.)

CREUSA

So it will be! So it will be!

And now   425

if Phoebus at last amends his former wrongs,
although he'll never be a friend for me,
I will accept, because he is a god,
whatever it is he chooses to bestow.

(Exit to the side.)

ION

Why does this stranger always speak in riddles,
reproach the god with covert blasphemy?   430
Is it through love of her on whose behalf
she comes before the oracle? Or does
she hide a secret which she cannot tell?
      But what concern have I with Erechtheus' daughter?
No, that is not my business.—I will pour
the holy water out of golden pitchers   435
into the lustral bowls. I must confront
Apollo with his wrongs. To force a girl
against her will and then abandon her!
To leave a child to die that has been born
in secret! No! Do not act thus. No, since
you have the power, seek the virtuous path.   440
All evil men are punished by the gods.
How then can it be just for you gods to stand
convicted of breaking laws you have yourselves
laid down for men? But if—here I suppose
what could not be—you gave account on earth
for wrongs which you have done to women, you,   445
Apollo, and Poseidon and Zeus who rules
in heaven, payment of your penalties
would see your temples empty, since you are
unjust to others in pursuing your pleasure
without forethought. And justice now demands
that we should say not men are wicked if   450
they imitate what the gods approve, but those
who teach men these things by their own example.

(*Exit to the side.*)

CHORUS [*singing*]

STROPHE

O my Athena, born
without birth pains,
brought forth from the head of Zeus
by Prometheus, the Titan, 455
blessed Goddess of Victory,
take wing from the golden halls
of Olympus, come, I entreat you,
here to the Pythian temple, 460
where at earth's center Apollo's shrine
proclaims unfailing prophecy,
at the tripod where they dance and sing.
Come with Artemis, Leto's daughter, 465
virgin goddesses both,
holy sisters of Phoebus.°
Beseech him, O maidens,
that the ancient family of Erechtheus may
at last be sure by a clear response 470
of the blessing of children.

ANTISTROPHE

Wherever gleams bright the flame
and strength of youth,
a promise to the house of growth,
there a man has a fund 475
of joy overflowing;
from the fathers the children will gather
hereditary wealth, and in turn
pass it on to their own. 480
They are a defense in adversity,
in happiness a delight,
and in war their country's shield of safety.
For myself I would choose, rather than wealth 485

or a palace of kings, to rear°
and love my own children:
shame to him who prefers
a childless life, hateful to me.
May I cling to the life of modest possessions,   490
enriched by children.

EPODE

O haunts of Pan,
the rock flanking
the caves of the Long Rocks,
where the three daughters of Aglaurus   495
dance, and their feet tread
the green levels before the shrines
of Pallas, in time to the changing
music of the pipes you play,   500
O Pan, in your sunless caves,
where a girl in misery
bore a child to Phoebus
and exposed it, a prey for birds,
food for wild beasts to rend, shame
of a cruel love.   505
Our legends, our tales at the loom,
never tell of good fortune to children
born of a god and a mortal.

(Enter Ion from the side.)

ION
   Serving women who are keeping watch here at the steps   510
   of the house of sacrifice, awaiting your master,
   tell me, has Xuthus already left the sacred tripod
   and the oracle, or does he still remain within,
   waiting for an answer to his childlessness?

CHORUS LEADER
   He is still inside. He has not passed this threshold yet.

But the noise the door has made shows someone is now
  there.   515
Look, it is my master coming out to us.

(Enter Xuthus from the temple. He runs excitedly up to Ion.)

XUTHUS

Son, my blessing.—It is right to greet you in this way.

ION

Sir, my thanks. We are both well—if you've not gone mad.

XUTHUS

Let me kiss your hand, allow me to embrace you.

ION

Are you sane? Or has the god made you mad somehow?   520

XUTHUS

Mad, when I've found my dearest love and want to touch
  him?

ION

Stop!—If you touch Apollo's garland, you may break it.

XUTHUS

I will touch you. And I am no robber. You are mine.

ION

Must I shoot this arrow first, or will you let me go?

XUTHUS

Why must you avoid me just when you have found your
  dearest?   525

ION

Mad and boorish strangers are no pleasure to instruct.

XUTHUS

Kill me, and then burn me. For you'll have killed your father.

ION

You my father! This is fool's talk.—How can that be? No!

XUTHUS

Yes.—The story which I have to tell will make it clear.

ION

What have you to say?

XUTHUS

I am your father. You are my son.   530

ION

Who has told you this?

XUTHUS

Apollo, he who reared my son.

ION

You are your own witness.

XUTHUS

Yes, I know what the oracle said.

ION

You mistook a riddle.

XUTHUS

Then my hearing must have failed.

ION

And what is Apollo's prophecy?

XUTHUS

That he whom I met . . .

ION

Oh! A meeting? Where?

XUTHUS

. . . as I came out of the temple here . . .   535

ION

Yes, and what would happen to him?

XUTHUS

... would be my son.

ION

Your own son or just a gift?

XUTHUS

A gift, but my own son.

ION

I was then the first you met?

XUTHUS

Yes, no one else, my son.

ION

But how strange this is!

XUTHUS

I am just as amazed as you.

ION

Well?—Who is my mother?

XUTHUS

That I cannot say.   540

ION

And Apollo?

XUTHUS

Happy with this news, I did not ask.

ION

Earth then was my mother!

XUTHUS

Children do not spring up from there.

ION

How could I be yours?

XUTHUS

                     Apollo, not I, has the answer.

ION

  Let us try another tack.

XUTHUS

                     Yes, that will help us more.

ION

  Did you have an affair outside marriage?

XUTHUS

                     Yes, in the folly of youth.   545

ION

  Before you were married?

XUTHUS

                     Yes, but never afterward.

ION

  So that could be my origin?

XUTHUS

                     The time at least agrees.

ION

  Then what am I doing here . . .

XUTHUS

                     I cannot tell you that.

ION

  . . . here, so far away?

XUTHUS

                     That is my puzzle too.

ION

  Have you been before to Delphi?

XUTHUS

To the wine god's torch feast.   550

ION

You stayed with a temple steward?

XUTHUS

He—there were girls of Delphi . . .

ION

He introduced you to their rites?

XUTHUS

Yes, Bacchus' maenads.

ION

You had drunk much?

XUTHUS

I was reveling in the wine god's feast.

ION

Then that was the time.

XUTHUS

And fate has found it out, my son.

ION

How did I get here?

XUTHUS

The girl perhaps exposed her child.   555

ION

I am not a slave then.

XUTHUS

And now accept your father.

ION

We surely must believe the god.

XUTHUS

That makes good sense.

ION

    Could I wish for better . . .

XUTHUS

                         Well, now you see things rightly.

ION

    . . . than descent from Zeus's son?

XUTHUS

                         This is indeed your birthright.

ION

    Shall I touch my father then?

XUTHUS

                         Yes, have faith in the god.   560

ION

    Father!

XUTHUS

                How dear is the sound of the name you have spoken!

ION

    We should both bless this day.

XUTHUS

                         It has brought me happiness.

ION

    My dear mother! Shall I ever see your face as well?
    Now, whoever you may be, I long to see you even
    more. But you are dead perhaps, and I can have no hope.   565

CHORUS LEADER

    We also share this house's happiness.
    Yet I could wish my mistress too might have
    the joy of children, and Erechtheus' race.

XUTHUS

    My son, Apollo rightly prophesied

that I should find you, and united us.   570
You found a father whom you never knew.
Your natural desire I share myself
that you will find your mother, I, in her
the woman who gave a son to me. And if
we leave all that to time, perhaps we shall   575
succeed. But end your waif's life in the temple.
Let me persuade you, come with me to Athens,
for there your father's prosperous power awaits°
you, and great wealth. You shall not have the name
of bastard and of beggar, but highborn   580
and well endowed with wealth. But why so silent?
Why hold your eyes downcast? Now you have changed
your father's joy to fear.

ION

Things have a different face as they appear   585
close to the eyes or far away. I bless
my fortune now that I have found a father.
But, father, listen to what is in my mind:
the earth-born people of glorious Athens are said
to be no immigrant race. I would intrude   590
there marked by two defects, a foreigner's son,
and myself a bastard. So if I remain
obscure, with this disgrace they will account
me nothing, nobody's son.° But if I aspire
to the city's helm, ambitious for a name,   595
I shall be hated by the powerless.
Superiority is always hated.
And those good men who can attain to wisdom
and keep their silence, since they are not eager
for public life, will mock my folly, in blindly   600
giving up peace and quiet for the risks of power.
And then if I invade positions which
are filled, I shall be countered by the votes
of those with knowledge who control affairs.

For so it always happens, father: men
who hold the cities and their dignities   605
above all are the enemies of their rivals.
     Then, coming to another's house as an immigrant,
to live with her who has no children, who
before had you to share the sorrow—now,
abandoned to a private grief, she will   610
have cause for bitterness and cause enough
to hate me when I take my place as heir:
without a child herself, she will not kindly
regard your own. Then you must either turn
to her, betraying me, or honor me   615
and throw your house into turmoil: for there is
no other way. How many wives have brought
their men to death with poison or the knife!
Then, childless, growing old, she has my pity.
For this affliction does not suit her birth.   620
     The praise of royalty itself is false—
a fair façade to hide the pain within.
What happiness or blessing has the man
who looks all around for violence, and fear
draws out his days? I would prefer to live   625
a happy citizen than be a king,
who must choose to have the evil as his friends,
and must abhor the good for fear of death.
You might reply that gold outweighs all this,
the joys of wealth—no joy for me to guard   630
a fortune, hear reproaches, suffer its pains.
Let me avoid distress, seek moderation.
     But father, hear the good points of my life
in Delphi: leisure first of all, most dear
to any man; the friendly people, no one   635
to thrust me rudely from my path—to yield,
give elbow room to those beneath me is
intolerable. Then I have been busy
with prayers to gods or talk with men,

serving the happy, not the discontented.
I've been receiving guests or sending them   640
off again, a fresh face always smiling
on fresh faces. I had what men should pray,
even against their will, to have: duty
and inclination both contrived to make
me righteous to god. When I compare the two,   645
father, I think I am more happy here.
Let me live here. Delight in magnificence
is not better than being content with little.

CHORUS LEADER
Well have you spoken, since indeed your words
mean happiness for her whom I do love.

XUTHUS
No more of this! Learn to enjoy success.   650
Let us inaugurate our life together
by holding here, where I have found my son,
a public banquet, and make the sacrifices
omitted at your birth. I will pretend
to bring you to my house as guest, and give
a feast for you; and then take you along   655
with me to Athens, not as my son but as
a visitor. I do not want to hurt
my childless wife with my own happiness.
But when I think the time is ripe, I will
persuade my wife to give consent to your
assumption of my rule over the land.   660
          Your name shall be Ion, a name that fits
your destiny; you were the first to meet
me as I came from Apollo's shrine.° But now
collect your friends together, say farewell
with feast and sacrifice, before you leave   665
this town of Delphi. And, you women slaves,
I order you, say nothing of our plans.
To tell my wife anything will mean your death.

ION

Yes, I will go. But one piece of good luck
eludes me still: unless I find my mother,
my life is worthless. If I may do so,   670
I pray my mother is Athenian,
so that through her I may have rights of speech.
For when a foreigner comes into a city
of pure blood, though in name a citizen,
his mouth's a slave: he has no right of speech.   675

(They exit to the side.)

CHORUS [*singing*]

STROPHE

I see tears and mourning
    triumphant, the beginning of sorrows,
    when the queen hears of the son,
    the blessing bestowed on her husband
    alone, still childless herself.   680
O Leto's prophetic son, what reply have you chanted?
    From where came this child, reared
    in your temple, and who is his mother?
    This oracle does not please me.
        There may be a fraud.   685
        I fear the issue
        of this encounter.
    For these are strange prophecies,   690
    telling me strange things.
    Treachery and chance combine
    in this boy of an alien blood.
        Who will deny it?

ANTISTROPHE

My friends, shall we clearly   695
    cry out in the ears of my mistress
    blame upon the husband who alone°
    afforded her hope she could share?
    Now he is happy, she is maimed by troubles.

She is falling to gray age; he does not honor his love.   700
  A stranger he came, wretch,
  to the house, and betrays the fortune
  bestowed. He wronged her.—Die then!
   And may he not gain
   from god the prayer   705
   he sends with holy cakes
  ablaze on bright altars.
  He shall be sure of my feelings,°
  how much I love the queen.   710
  The new father and son are now near
   to their new banquet.

EPODE

O the ridge of the rocks of Parnassus
which hold in the skies the watchtower   715
where Dionysus holds the two-flamed
torch, leaping lightly with his
nighttime wandering maenads:
  let the boy never see my city,
  let him die first, leave his new life.   720
  A city in trouble has reason°
  to welcome the coming of strangers.
  But Erechtheus, our ancient founder,
   united us long ago.

(Enter Creusa and the Old Man from the side.)

CREUSA

Old man, my father, Erechtheus, while he was   725
alive already had you as his tutor:
come up with me now to Phoebus' oracle
to share my happiness if his prophecy
gives hope of children; since it is a joy
to share success with those we love; and if—   730
I pray that they may not—reverses come,
there is comfort in seeing a friendly face.

And, though I'm your mistress, I care for you as if
you were my father, as you did my own.

OLD MAN

    My daughter, you preserve a noble spirit   735
    and equal to your noble ancestors:
    you do not shame your fathers, sons of Earth.
    Give me your help, and bring me to the temple.
    The shrine is steep, you know. Support my limbs
    and heal my weak old age.   740

CREUSA

    Come then. Be careful how you place your feet.

OLD MAN

    You see. My mind is nimbler than my feet.

CREUSA

    Lean on your staff as the path winds around.

OLD MAN

    The staff is blind too when my eyes are weak.

CREUSA

    Yes, true. But fight against your weariness.   745

OLD MAN

    I do. But now I have no strength to summon.

CREUSA

    You women, faithful servants of my loom
    and shuttle, what hope of children did my husband
    receive before he left? We came for that.
    Tell me; and if the news is good you will   750
    not find your mistress faithless or ungrateful.

CHORUS LEADER [*singing*]

    An evil fate!

OLD MAN

    Your prelude is not one that suits good luck.

CHORUS LEADER [*singing*]
　Unhappy lot!

OLD MAN
　But what is wrong about the oracle?　　　　　　　　

CHORUS LEADER [*now speaking*]
　What can we do when death is set before us?

CREUSA
　What strain is this? Why should you be afraid?

CHORUS LEADER
　Are we to speak or not? What shall we do?

CREUSA
　O speak! You know of some misfortune coming.

CHORUS LEADER
　You shall be told then, even if I die　　　　　　　　
　twice over.—You will never have a child
　to hold in your arms, or take one to your breast.

CREUSA [*singing in a lyric interchange with the Old Man, who also sings
in reply*]
　I wish I were dead.

OLD MAN
　Daughter!

CREUSA
　　　　　　*O this blow
　　　is hard, this pain put upon me,
　　　I cannot endure it, my friends.*

OLD MAN
　Hopeless now, my child.

CREUSA
　　　　　　Yes, ah! Yes.　　　　　　　　
　　　*This blow is fatal, a heart-thrust.
　　　The sorrow has pierced within.*

OLD MAN [*now speaking*]
Mourn no more . . .

CREUSA [*continuing to sing throughout this scene*]
I have reason enough.

OLD MAN
. . . until we know . . .

CREUSA
Is there anything to know?   770

OLD MAN
. . . if you alone have this misfortune, or
my master too must share the same distress.

CHORUS LEADER
To him Apollo gave a son, but this
good luck is his alone; his wife has nothing.   775

CREUSA
One after the other you have cried out my griefs.
This is the worst to lament.

OLD MAN
And did the oracle concern a living son,
or must some woman yet give birth to him?

CHORUS LEADER
Loxias gave him a son already born,   780
a full-grown youth; and I myself was witness.

CREUSA
How can it be true? No! An incredible thing.
It is unspeakable.

OLD MAN
Unspeakable indeed! Tell me how the oracle   785
is being fulfilled, and who the son can be.

[247] ION

CHORUS LEADER

He gave your husband for a son the one
he would meet first as he came from the temple.

CREUSA

Ah, ah! Then it is settled.
He said mine is the childless part,   790
the solitary life in a desolate house.

OLD MAN

Who then was destined for Xuthus to meet?
And tell me how and where he saw his child.

CHORUS LEADER

There was a young man who swept the temple here.
You know him, lady? That one is the son.   795

CREUSA

I wish that I might fly
through the moist air far away
from Greek earth to the western stars!
Such is my anguish, my friends.

OLD MAN

What was the name his father gave to him?   800
You know it? Or does that remain uncertain?

CHORUS LEADER

He called him Ion, since he met him first.°
But who his mother is°—that I cannot say.
Xuthus, to tell you all I know, old man,
has gone away unbeknownst to her, his wife,
to offer in the consecrated tent   805
a birthday sacrifice, to pledge the bond
of friendship in a feast with his new son.

OLD MAN

My lady, we have been betrayed—I share
in your grief—by that man, your husband. We are

insulted by design, cast from Erechtheus'   810
house: I say this not because I hate him,
but rather because I love you more than him—
the foreigner who arrived and married you,
was welcomed to the city and your house,
received your heritage, and now is proved the father
of children by another woman—secretly.   815
How secretly I will explain to you.
Aware that you yourself would have no children,
he scorned to suffer equally with you
in this mischance, and had a secret child
by some slave woman, and then sent him away
for someone here in Delphi to rear. The boy   820
was dedicated to Apollo's temple,
and there grew in concealment. Then the father,
now knowing that the boy was grown, pressed you
to travel here because you had no child.
And it wasn't Apollo who lied, but this man, who   825
has long been rearing the child. This is his web
of deceit: discovered, he would lay the blame
upon the god; if not, to guard against°
the blows of time, his plan was to invest
him with the city's rule. As time went on,
the new name Ion was invented, suiting   830
this trick of meeting him outside the temple.

CHORUS LEADER

I hate all evil men who plot injustice,
then trick it out with subterfuge. I would
prefer as friend a good man ignorant
than one more clever who is evil too.   835

OLD MAN

Worst shame of all that he should bring into
your house a cipher, motherless, the child
of some slave woman. For the shame at least
would have been single, if, with your consent,

because you could not bear a child yourself,   840
he had an heir by one highborn. If this
had been too much, he should have been content
to marry an Aeolian.
          And so you now must act a woman's part:
kill them, your husband and his son, by sword,°
by poison, or some trick, before death comes   845
to you from them. Unless you act, your life
is lost; for when two enemies have met
together in one house, then one must be
the loser. Now I'll help you kill the son: 850
visiting the place where he prepares the feast,
to pay the debt I owe my masters thus,
and then to live or die. A slave bears only this
disgrace: the name. In every other way   855
an honest slave is equal to the free.

CHORUS LEADER
  I too, dear mistress, want to share your fate,
  to die with you, or else to live with honor.

CREUSA [singing]
  O my heart, how be silent?
  Yet how can I speak of that secret   860
  love, strip myself of all shame?
  [chanting]
  Is one barrier left still to prevent me?
  Whom have I now as my rival in virtue?
  Has not my husband become my betrayer?
  I am cheated of home, cheated of children,   865
  hopes are gone which I could not fulfill,
  the hopes of arranging things well
  by hiding the rape,
  by hiding the birth which brought sorrow.
  No! No! But I swear by the starry abode   870
  of Zeus, by the goddess who reigns on our peaks
  and by the sacred shore of the lake

of Tritonis, I will no longer conceal that rape:
when I have put away the burden,
my heart will be easier.   875
Tears fall from my eyes, and my spirit is sick,
evilly plotted against by men and by gods;
I will expose them,
ungrateful betrayers of women's beds.   880

[singing]
O you who give the seven-toned lyre
a voice which rings out of the lifeless,
rustic horn the lovely sound
of the Muses' hymns,
on you, Leto's son, here   885
in daylight I will lay blame.
You came with hair flashing
gold, as I gathered
into my cloak saffron flowers ablaze
with the golden light.   890
Grabbing my pale wrists
as I cried for my mother's help
you led me to bed in a cave,
a god and my lover, shamelessly   895
gratifying the Cyprian goddess's will.
In misery I bore you
a son, whom in fear of my mother
I placed in that bed
where you cruelly forced me.   900
Ah! He is lost now,
snatched as food for birds,
my son and yours; O lost!
        But you play the lyre,   905
            singing your paeans.
Oh, O hear me, son of Leto,
who assign your prophecies
from the golden throne

and the temple at earth's center,   910
I will proclaim my words to the daylight:
ah, ah! you are an evil lover;
though you owed no favor
to my husband, you have
set a son in his house.   915
But my son, yes and yours, hard-hearted,°
is lost, carried away by birds,
the swaddling clothes his mother put on him abandoned.
    Delos hates you, and the young
    laurel which grows by the palm   920
    with its delicate leaves, where Leto
    bore you, a holy child, fruit of Zeus.

CHORUS LEADER

O what a store of miseries is now
disclosed; who would not weep at hearing them?

OLD MAN

O child, watching your face I'm filled with pity°   925
and my reason is distracted. For just when
I banished from my heart one wave of trouble,
a second one rose at the stern, caused by the words
you spoke about your present woes, before
you trod the evil path of other sorrows.   930
What do you say? What is your accusation
against Apollo? What child is this you claim
you bore? Where in the city did you put
this beloved corpse for beasts? Tell me again.

CREUSA

I will tell you, although I feel ashamed.

OLD MAN

Yes, I know how to feel with friends in trouble.   935

CREUSA

Then listen. You know the northern cave which lies
above the hill of Cecrops, called Long Rocks?

OLD MAN

I know. Pan's altars and his shrine are near.

CREUSA

It was there that I endured a fearful trial.

OLD MAN

Yes? My tears well up to meet your words.   940

CREUSA

Phoebus became my lover against my will.

OLD MAN

My child, could that have been the thing I noticed?

CREUSA

What was it? Speak out, and I'll tell the truth.

OLD MAN

When you were suffering from a secret illness?

CREUSA

That was the sorrow which I now reveal.   945

OLD MAN

How did you hide this union with Apollo?

CREUSA

I had a child.—Please hear my story out.

OLD MAN

But where? Who helped you? Or were you alone?

CREUSA

Alone in that cave where I met Apollo.

OLD MAN

Where is the child? You need not be childless.   950

CREUSA

Dead. He was left for beasts to prey upon.

OLD MAN

Dead? Then Phoebus was false, gave you no help?

CREUSA

He did not help. The child grows up in Hades.

OLD MAN

But who exposed the child? Of course not you?

CREUSA

I did: I wrapped him in my robes at night.   955

OLD MAN

And there was no accomplice in your deed?

CREUSA

No, nothing but concealment and misfortune.

OLD MAN

How could you leave your child there, in the cave?

CREUSA

How, but with many tender words of pity?

OLD MAN

Ah, you were harsh; Apollo harsher still.   960

CREUSA

If you'd seen the child stretch out his hands to me!

OLD MAN

To find your breast, or to lie there in your arms?

CREUSA

Yes, to find what I was cruelly refusing.

OLD MAN

But why did you decide to expose your child?

CREUSA

Because I hoped the god would save his own.   965

OLD MAN

Ah, what a storm embroils your house's fortunes!

CREUSA

Why do you hide your head, old man, and weep?

OLD MAN

I see your father and yourself so stricken.

CREUSA

Such is the life of mortals. All things change.

OLD MAN

My child, let us no longer cling to tears.   970

CREUSA

What can I do? For pain has no resource.

OLD MAN

Avenge yourself on the god, who wronged you first.

CREUSA

How can a mortal fight immortal power?

OLD MAN

Burn down Apollo's sacred oracle.

CREUSA

I am afraid. I have enough of sorrow.   975

OLD MAN

Then do what's in your power: kill your husband.

CREUSA

He was once loyal, and I honor that.

OLD MAN

Then kill the son, who's come to menace you.

CREUSA

But how? If only I might! I would do that!

OLD MAN

By putting swords into your attendants' hands.   980

CREUSA

Let us begin. But where can it be done?

OLD MAN

The sacred tent, where he is feasting friends.

CREUSA

Murder is flagrant; slaves are weak support.

OLD MAN

Ah, you're being a coward; come now, make a plan!

CREUSA

Well yes, I have something which is sure and subtle.   985

OLD MAN

And I can be your helper in both these ways.

CREUSA

Then listen. You know the war fought by Earth's sons?

OLD MAN

When the Giants fought against the gods at Phlegra.

CREUSA

Earth there produced an awful monster, Gorgon.

OLD MAN

To help her children and harass the gods?   990

CREUSA

Yes, but killed by Zeus's daughter Pallas.°   991

OLD MAN

Is this the tale which I have heard before?   994

CREUSA

Yes, that she wears its skin upon her breast.   995

OLD MAN

Athena's armor which they call her aegis?   996

CREUSA

So called from how she rushed into the battle.   997

OLD MAN

What is the appearance of this ferocious thing?   992

CREUSA

A breastplate that is armed with serpent coils.   993

OLD MAN

But my child, what harm can this do to your foes?   998

CREUSA

You know Erichthonius?—Of course you must.

OLD MAN

The founder of your house, the son of Earth.   1000

CREUSA

To him, as a newborn child, Athena gave . . .

OLD MAN

Yes, what is this you hesitate to say?

CREUSA

. . . two drops from the blood of the Gorgon.

OLD MAN

And what is their effect on human beings?

CREUSA

The one is poisonous, the other cures disease.   1005

OLD MAN

But how did she attach them to the child?

CREUSA

By golden chains which he gave to my father.

OLD MAN

And then, when he had died, it came to you?

CREUSA

Yes, I always wear it on my wrist.

OLD MAN

How is the twofold gift compounded then?   1010

CREUSA

The drop extracted from its hollow vein . . .

OLD MAN

How is it to be used? What power has it?

CREUSA

. . . fosters life and keeps away disease.

OLD MAN

What action does the other of them have?

CREUSA

It kills—a poison from the Gorgon's snakes.   1015

OLD MAN

You carry them apart or mixed together?

CREUSA

Apart. For good and evil do not mingle.

OLD MAN

O my dear child, you have all that you need!

CREUSA

By this the boy shall die, and you shall kill him.

OLD MAN

But when and how? Tell me: it shall be done.   1020

CREUSA

In Athens when he comes into my house.

OLD MAN

No, I distrust this plan as you did mine.

CREUSA

Why?—Can we both have seen the same weak point?

OLD MAN

They will accuse you, innocent or guilty.

CREUSA

True: they say stepmothers are always jealous.   1025

OLD MAN

So kill him here and then deny the crime.

CREUSA

And in that way I taste my joy the sooner.

OLD MAN

And turn his own deceit upon your husband.

CREUSA

You know then what you are to do? Here, take
this golden bracelet from my hand, Athena's   1030
old gift; go where my husband holds his feast
in secret; when they end the meal, begin
to pour the gods' libation, then drop this,
under the cover of your robe, into
the young man's cup—in his alone, not all.   1035
Reserve the drink for him who would assume
the mastery of my home. Once he drains this,
he will be dead and here is where he'll stay—
never will he see our glorious Athens.

OLD MAN

Now go to your host's house, and I will do
the task that I have been assigned to do.   1040
        Old feet, come now, take on a youthful strength
for work, although the years deny it you.
March with your mistress upon the enemy,

and help to kill and cast him from the house.
It's right that the fortunate should honor piety,   1045
but when we wish to harm our enemies
there is no law which can get in our way.

(*Exit Creusa to one side and the Old Man to the other.*)

CHORUS [*singing*]

STROPHE A

Demeter's daughter, guarding the roadway, ruling
what moves through the paths of the night
and the daytime, O guide the filling   1050
of the death-heavy cup
to whom the queen sends it, brew
of the blood-drops from the Gorgon's severed throat,   1055
to him who lifts his presumptuous hand
against the house of Erechtheus.
        Let none from other houses have
        sway in the city:
        only the sons of Erechtheus.   1060

ANTISTROPHE A

My mistress is planning a death, and if it should fail,
the occasion of action go past,
now her sole anchor of hope,
she will sharpen a sword
or fasten a noose to her neck,   1065
ending sorrow by sorrows, pass down to a different life.
For she would never endure to see
foreigners ruling the house,   1070
        not while, living, her eyes°
        still have their clarity—
        she, born of a noble line.

STROPHE B

O the shame to many-hymned Dionysus,
if by the springs of Callichoroe   1075
Apollo's wandering boy shall behold

unsleeping, keeping the watch,
the torches burning on the festival night,
when the star-faced heavens join in the dance,   1080
with the moon and the fifty Nereids
who dance in the depths of the sea,°
in perennial river-springs,
honoring the gold-crowned Maid   1085
and her mother, holy Demeter:
    there, where he hopes
    to rule, usurping
    what others have wrought.

ANTISTROPHE B

All you poets who raise your unjust strains   1090
singing the unsanctioned, unholy loves
of women, see how much we surpass
in virtue the unrighteous race   1095
of men. Let a song of different strain
ring out against men, harshly indicting°
their loves. For here is one
of the offspring of Zeus's sons who shows
his ingratitude, failing   1100
to bring good luck to the house
with his and Creusa's child:
    but yielding to passion
    for another, he has
    a bastard son.   1105

(Enter a Servant of Creusa from the side.)

SERVANT
  Women, can you tell me where I may find
  Erechtheus' noble daughter?° I have searched
  the city everywhere without success.

CHORUS LEADER
  What is it, friend? Why are you hurrying?
  What is the message you have brought?   1110

SERVANT

    They're after us. The Delphians are looking
    for her to stone her to death.

CHORUS LEADER

    What do you mean? Have they discovered then
    the secret plot we made to kill the boy?

SERVANT

    Correct—and you will not be the last to suffer.   1115

CHORUS LEADER

    How was this scheme, unknown to them, discovered?

SERVANT

    The god refused to be defiled,° and so
    discovered how justice could defeat injustice.

CHORUS LEADER

    But how? I beg you tell me that: for whether
    I have to die, or not, I shall be more   1120
    content if I can know just what has happened.

SERVANT

    Creusa's husband came out from the shrine
    of Phoebus, and then took his new-found son
    away to join the feast and sacrifice
    he was preparing for the gods. Xuthus
    himself was going to the place where   1125
    the sacred Bacchanalian fires leap,
    to sprinkle the twin crags of Dionysus
    with victims' blood for having seen his son.
    "My son," he said, "will you stay here and see
    that workmen build a tent enclosed on all
    its sides? And if I should be long away,
    while sacrificing to the gods of birth,   1130
    begin the banquet with such friends as come."
         He took the sacrificial calves and left.
    Ion had the framework built in ritual form

on upright poles without a wall, and paid
attention to the sun, so that he might   1135
avoid its midday and its dying rays
of flame, and measuring a square, its sides
a hundred feet, so that he could invite
all Delphi to the feast. To shade the tent   1140
he took from store some sacred tapestries,
a wonder to behold. And first he shaded
the roof-frame with a wing of cloth, spoil from
the Amazons, which Heracles, the son
of Zeus, had dedicated to the god.   1145
And there were figures woven in design:
for Ouranus was mustering the stars
in heaven's circle; and Helios drove his horses
toward his dying flame and trailed the star
which shines bright in the West. While black-robed Night,   1150
drawn by a pair, urged on her chariot,
beside her the stars kept pace. The Pleiades
and Orion, his sword in hand, moved through
the sky's midpath; and over them, the Bear
who turned his golden tail around the Pole.
The round full moon threw up her rays, dividing   1155
the month; the Hyades, the guide most sure
for sailors; then light's herald, Dawn, routing
the stars. The sides he draped with tapestries
also, these of barbarian design.
There were fine ships which fought with Greeks, and
     creatures,   1160
half man, half beast, and horsemen chasing deer
or lion hunts. And at the entrance, Cecrops,
his daughters near him, wreathed himself in coils
of serpents—this a gift which had been given
by some Athenian. Then in the center   1165
he put the golden mixing bowls. A herald
rose up then and announced that any Delphian
who pleased was free to attend the feast. And when

the tent was full, they wreathed their heads with flowers
and ate the food spread in abundance till
desire was satisfied.
                          When they had done   1170
with eating,° an old man came in and stood
among the guests, and threw them into laughter
with his officious antics. He poured out
water from jars to wash their hands, or burned
the ooze of myrrh, and put himself in charge   1175
of golden drinking cups. And when the reed pipes
joined in, together with the mixing bowl which all
had now to drink, he said, "Enough of these
small cups, we must have large; the company
will then be all the sooner in good spirits."   1180
And now they busied themselves with passing gold
and silver cups; but he, as though he meant
to honor his new master, offered him
a special cup, full of wine, in which
he had dropped a fatal poison which they say   1185
our mistress had given, to eliminate this new son.
And no one saw. But when like all the rest
Ion held his cup, one of the slaves let fall
some phrase of evil omen. Ion had been reared
among good prophets in the temple, and knew   1190
the sign and ordered them to fill another.
The first libation of the god he emptied
on the ground and told the rest to pour
as he had done. A silence followed as
we filled the sacred bowls with Bibline wine   1195
and water. While this was being done, there came
into the tent a riotous flight of doves—
they haunt Apollo's shrine and have no fear.
To slake their thirst, they dipped their beaks into
the wine the guests had poured and drew it down   1200
their well-plumed throats; and all but one were not
harmed by the god's libation. But one had perched

where Ion poured his wine, and tasted it.
At once her feathered body shook and quivered,
maenad-like, she screamed strange cries of anguish.   1205
The guests all watched, amazed to see her struggles.
She died in her convulsions, her pink claws
and legs gone limp. The son the god foretold
then stretched his uncloaked arms across the table,
and cried, "Who planned my death? Tell me, old man,   1210
since you were so officious; you handed me
the drink." He held the old man by the arm
and searched him instantly, so that he might
convict him in the act.° His guilt was proved
and he revealed, compelled against his will,   1215
Creusa's plotting with the poisoned drink.
        The youth bestowed by Loxias collected
the guests, went from the tent without delay,
and took his stand before the Delphian nobles.
"O rulers of the sacred city," he said,   1220
"a foreign woman, daughter of Erechtheus,
has tried to poison me." The lords of Delphi
by many votes decided that my mistress
be put to death, thrown from the rock, for planning
the murder of a sacred person there
inside the temple. Now all the city's looking   1225
for her whom misery advanced on this
unhappy path. Desire for children caused
her visit here to Phoebus, but now her life
is lost, and with her life all hopes of children.

CHORUS [*singing*]
There is no escape, we are doomed,
no escape from death.   1230
It has been made clear,
by the libation of Dionysian grapes°
mingled for murder with blood drops
from the swift-working viper,

clear that in sacrifice to the gods below   1235
my life is set for disaster,
and they will stone my mistress to death.
What winged flight can I take,
down to what dark caverns of the earth
can I go to escape the stones of destruction?   1240
By mounting a chariot
drawn by horses with speedy hooves,
or the prow of a ship?

[chanting]
There is no concealment, unless a god wishes
to withdraw us from sight.   1245
O unhappy mistress, what sufferings
wait for your soul? Shall we not,
because we intended to do harm to our fellows,
according to justice, suffer ourselves?

                                        (Enter Creusa from the side.)

CREUSA
They are in pursuit, my friends; they want to kill me;   1250
by the judgment of the Pythian vote my life is forfeit.

CHORUS LEADER
Yes, we know in what distress you are, unhappy woman.

CREUSA
Where can I find refuge then? For I have evaded them
by a trick, just left the house in time to save my life.

CHORUS LEADER
Where, but at the altar?

CREUSA
                                What advantage will that give me?   1255

CHORUS LEADER
God defends the suppliant.

CREUSA
                                Yes, but the law condemns me.

CHORUS LEADER

They must seize you first.

CREUSA

And here my bitter adversaries come,
pressing on with sword in hand.

CHORUS LEADER

Sit on the altar now.
For if you die sitting there, your killers will be made
guilty of your blood. Your fate must be endured.   1260

(Enter Ion from the side, with a group of armed Delphians.)

ION

O Cephisus, bull-shaped ancestor,
what viper or what serpent glancing out
its deadly flame of fire did you beget
in her, this woman who will balk at nothing,
worse than the Gorgon drops with which she tried   1265
to poison me! Take hold of her and let
Parnassus' peaks dishevel those perfect tresses,
when like a ball she's bounced from rock to rock.
    Luck favored me before I went to Athens
to fall a victim to a stepmother.   1270
For here, among my friends I learned to measure
your mind, your menace, and your enmity.
But if I had been trapped inside your house,
you would have sent me utterly to death.

(Creusa runs to the altar and sits on it.)

The altar will not save you, nor Apollo's°   1275
house, since much greater pity is reserved
for me and for my mother. For even if
in body she's not here, her name's not absent.

(To his companions.)

You see her treachery—how she can twist

one scheme upon another! She has fled
to cower at the god's own altar, hoping   1280
thus to avoid her penalty for wrong.

CREUSA
I warn you not to kill me—and I speak
not only for myself but for the god
who guards this place.

ION
What can you have in common with the god?

CREUSA
My body is his to save, a sacred charge.   1285

ION
You tried to poison me and I was his.

CREUSA
No longer his; for you had found your father.

ION
I belonged to Phoebus till my father came.°

CREUSA
But then no more. Now I belong to him.

ION
Yes, but I had the piety you lack.   1290

CREUSA
I tried to kill the enemy of my house.

ION
I did not march upon your land with arms.

CREUSA
Yes you did, and you tried to burn Erechtheus' house!

ION
What fiery flame, what torches did I carry?

CREUSA

You hoped to force possession of my home.   1295

ION

My father's gift—the land he gained himself.

CREUSA

How can Aeolians share Athenian land?

ION

Because he saved it, not with words, but arms.

CREUSA

An ally need not own the land he helps!

ION

You planned my death through fear of my intentions?°   1300

CREUSA

To save my life if you stopped just intending.

ION

Childless yourself, you envied my father's child.

CREUSA

So you will snatch those homes without an heir?

ION

Had I no right to share my father's land?

CREUSA

A shield and spear, these are your sole possessions.   1305

ION

Come, leave the altar and the shrine of god.

CREUSA

Go, find your mother, and give her your advice.

ION

While your attempted murder goes unpunished?

CREUSA

Not if you wish to kill me in the shrine.

ION

What pleasure can the god's wreaths give to death?   1310

CREUSA

I shall thus injure one who injured me.

ION

O this is monstrous! The laws of god for men
are not well made, their judgment is unwise.
The unjust should not have the right of refuge
at altars, but be driven away. For gods   1315
are soiled by the touch of wicked hands. The just,
the injured party, should have this asylum.
Instead both good and bad alike all come,
receiving equal treatment from the gods.

(Enter the Priestess of Apollo from the temple, carrying a cradle.)

PRIESTESS

O stop, my son. For I, the prophetess   1320
of Phoebus, chosen from all the Delphian women
to keep the tripod's ancient law, have left
the seat of prophecy to pass these bounds.

ION

Dear mother, hail! Mother in all but birth.

PRIESTESS

Then let me be so called. It pleases me.   1325

ION

You heard how she had planned to murder me?

PRIESTESS

I heard—but your own cruelty is sinful.

ION

Have I no right to kill a murderer?

PRIESTESS

Wives are unkind to children not their own.

ION

As we can be to them if they mistreat us.   1330

PRIESTESS

No. When you leave the temple for your country . . .

ION

What must I do? What is your advice?

PRIESTESS

. . . go into Athens, pure and with good omens.

ION

All men are pure who kill their enemies.

PRIESTESS

No more of that. Hear what I have to say.   1335

ION

Then speak. Your message could not be unfriendly.

PRIESTESS

You see the basket I am carrying?

ION

I see an ancient cradle bound with wool.

PRIESTESS

I found you in this once, a newborn child.

ION

What do you say? This tale is new to me.   1340

PRIESTESS

I kept it secret. Now I can reveal it.

ION

Why did you keep it from me all these years?

PRIESTESS

The god desired to keep you as his servant.

ION

And now he does not wish it? How can I know?

PRIESTESS

Revealing your father, he bids you go from here.   1345

ION

Why did you keep the cradle? Was that an order?

PRIESTESS

Apollo put the thought into my mind . . .

ION

What thought? Tell me. I want to hear the end.

PRIESTESS

. . . to keep what I had found until this time.

ION

And does it bring me any help?—or harm?   1350

PRIESTESS

The swaddling clothes you wore are kept inside.

ION

These clues you bring will help to find my mother?

PRIESTESS

The god desires this now—though not before.

ION

This is indeed a day of happy signs!

(She gives him the cradle.)

PRIESTESS

Take this with you—and now look for your mother.   1355

ION

Throughout all Asia, beyond the bounds of Europe!

PRIESTESS

That is your own affair. I reared you, child,

by Phoebus' will, and give these back to you,
what he wished me to take and keep, although
without express command.° Why he so wished   1360
I cannot say. There was no man who knew
that I had these or where they were concealed.
And now farewell. I kiss you like a mother.
As for the search, begin it as you ought:°
your mother might have been a Delphian girl   1365
who left you at the temple; inquire here first,
and then elsewhere in Greece. Now you have heard
all that we have to say—Apollo, who had
an interest in your fate, and I myself.

                              (*Exit into the temple.*)

ION

O how the tears well from my eyes whenever
my mind goes back to that time when the woman   1370
who gave me birth, the child of secret love,
disposed of me by stealth, and kept me from
her breast. Instead, unnamed, I had a life
of service in Apollo's house. My fate
was cruel, though the god was kind. I was
deprived of my dear mother's love throughout
the time I might have lived content and happy,   1375
held in her arms. My mother suffered too;
she lost the joy a child can bring.
                                        And now
I will consign the cradle as a gift   1380
to god to ward away unpleasant news.
If by some chance my mother were a slave,
to find her would be worse than ignorance.
O Phoebus, to your shrine I dedicate it.
            And yet, what am I doing? It is against   1385
the god's own wish; he has preserved for me
my mother's tokens. I must have the courage
to open them. I cannot shun my fate.

O sacred bands and ties which guard my precious
tokens, what secret do you hide from me?   1390

                                    (He examines the cradle.)

A miracle! See how the cradle's covering
is still unworn; the wicker is not decayed,
yet years have passed since they were put away.

CREUSA

But what is this I see—beyond my hopes?   1395

ION

Silence. You were my enemy before.

CREUSA

This is no time for silence. Do not try
to check me. In that cradle I exposed
you then, O my own son, a newborn child,
where the Long Rocks hang over Cecrops' cave.   1400
I will desert this altar even if
I have to die.

                                    (She leaves the altar and runs up to Ion.)

ION

Seize her! God's madness has made her leap away
from the altar's images. Now bind her arms.

CREUSA

Go on and kill me. I'll compete with her
and you for what is hidden there inside.   1405

ION

Is not this dreadful? To rob me with a trick!

CREUSA

No! You are found, a loved one for your loved ones.

ION

What, you love me? And try a secret murder?

CREUSA

You are my son: what's most loved by his parents.

ION

Stop spinning lies. For I am sure to catch you.   1410

CREUSA

O do so then! That is my aim, my son.

ION

This cradle—has it anything inside?

CREUSA

It has the clothes you wore when I exposed you.

ION

And can you give their names before you see them?

CREUSA

I can; and, if I fail, I agree to die.   1415

ION

Then speak. Your audacity is strange indeed.

CREUSA

Look, all, at weaving which I did in childhood.

ION

Describe it; girls weave many kinds of things.

CREUSA

It is unfinished, a kind of trial piece.

ION

And its design? You cannot cheat me there.   1420

CREUSA

There is a Gorgon in the center part.

ION

O Zeus! What fate is this that tracks me down!

CREUSA

The piece is fringed with serpents like an aegis.

ION

And here it is, found like an oracle!°

CREUSA

The loomwork of a girl—so long ago.   1425

ION

And anything else? Or will your luck fail now?

CREUSA

Serpents, all gold, our ancient race's custom.°

ION

Athena bids you raise your child in them?

CREUSA

Yes, in memory of Erichthonius.

ION

What do they do with this gold ornament?   1430

CREUSA

It is a necklace for a newborn child.

ION

Yes, here it is. I long to know what's third.

CREUSA

I put an olive wreath around you then,
from the first tree Athena's rock brought forth;
if that is there, it has not lost its green,   1435
but flourishes because the tree is holy.

ION

O dearest mother, what happiness to see you,
to kiss you, and to know that you are happy!

CREUSA

O child! O light more welcome than the sun!
—The god forgive me—I have you in my arms.   1440

[singing throughout this interchange with Ion, who speaks in reply]
I have found you against all my hopes,
whom I thought underground in the world
of Persephone's shades.

ION

Dear mother, yes, you have me in your arms,
who died and now have come to you alive.

CREUSA

O radiant heaven's expanse,   1445
how can I speak or cry
my joy? How have I met
unimagined delight, and what
has made me happy?

ION

There was no more unlikely chance than this,   1450
to find that I am, after all, your son.

CREUSA

I am trembling with fear.

ION

That I'd be lost, although you hold me now?

CREUSA

Yes, since I had cast all hope away.
But tell me, priestess, from where
did you take my child to your arms?
Whose hand brought him to Apollo's house?   1455

ION

It was the work of god. But as we have suffered
before, so now we must enjoy our fortune.

CREUSA

My child, you were born in tears,
in sorrow torn from your mother.
But now I can breathe on your cheek,   1460
and am blessed with tender joy.

ION

I have no need to speak. You speak for both.

CREUSA

I am childless no longer,
no longer without an heir.
The hearth is restored to the home,
the rulers return to the land,
And Erechtheus is young once more;   1465
now the house of the earth-born is delivered from night
and looks up to the rays of the sun.

ION

Mother, my father should be here with me
to share the happiness I bring you both.

CREUSA

My child, my child,   1470
how am I put to shame!

ION

Yes? Tell me.

CREUSA

You do not know your father.

ION

So I'm a bastard, born before your marriage?

CREUSA

The marriage which gave you birth
saw no torches or dancing, my son.   1475

ION

A lowly birth! Mother, who was my father?

CREUSA

Athena who slew the Gorgon,
I call her to witness ...

ION

Why this beginning?

CREUSA

... she who on my cliff
sits upon the hill that bears olives ...

ION

Your words to me are cryptic and obscure.

CREUSA

... by the rocks where the nightingales sing,   1480
Apollo—

ION

Why name Apollo?

CREUSA

... became my lover in secret ...

ION

Speak on; for what you say will make me happy.   1485

CREUSA

... and when nine months passed, I bore you,
the unknown child of Apollo.

ION

How welcome this news is, if it is true!

CREUSA

And these were your swaddling clothes;
in fear° of my mother I wrapped you   1490
in them, the careless work of a girl
at her loom.
I gave you no milk;
you were not washed with my hands,
but in a deserted cave,
a prey for the beaks of birds,   1495
delivered to death.

ION

O mother, what horror you dared!

CREUSA

Myself in the bondage of fear,
I was casting away your life,
I killed you against my will.°

ION

And I attempted an impious murder.°   1500

CREUSA

    Fate drove us hard in the past,
    just now oppressed us again.
    There is no harbor of peace
from the changing waves of joy and despair.   1505
    The wind's course veers.
    Let it rest. We have endured
    sorrows enough. O my son,
    pray for a favoring breeze
        of rescue from trouble.

CHORUS LEADER

From what we have seen happen here, no man   1510
should ever think that anything is hopeless.

ION

O Fortune, you've transformed unnumbered lives
to misery and then again to joy!
How near I was to killing my own mother,
how near myself to undeserved disaster.   1515
But don't the sun's bright rays in daily course
illumine many such events as this?
It was so good at last to find you, mother,
and I can cast no blame upon my birth.
But there is something else I wish to say   1520
to you alone. Come here with me; my words
are for your ear; your answer shall be hidden.

Now tell me, mother—might you not, deceived
as young girls are in love affairs kept secret,
be laying blame upon the god, and saying,   1525
attempting to escape the shame I brought,
that Phoebus is my father, though in fact
the one who fathered me was no god at all?

CREUSA [now speaking]
  No, by Athena, Goddess of Victory,
  who in her chariot fought by Zeus's side
  against the Giant race, my son, your father
  was not a mortal being but a god,   1530
  the very one who reared you, Loxias lord.

ION
  If this is true, why give his son to others,
  why does he say that Xuthus is my father?

CREUSA
  No, he does not; you are his son, a gift
  bestowed by him on Xuthus, just as a man   1535
  might give a friend his son to be his heir.

ION
  But, mother, does Apollo tell the truth,
  or is the oracle false? With some good reason
  that question does not cease to trouble me.

CREUSA
  Then listen. This is what I think, my son:
  it is for your own good that Loxias   1540
  is placing you within a noble house.
  Acknowledged as his son, you would have lost
  all hope of heritage or father's name.
  What chance did you have when I concealed
  the truth, and even planned your death in secret?
  And so to help you he is giving you
  another father.   1545

ION

My question cannot be so lightly answered;
no, I will ask Apollo in his temple
if I am a son of his, or born of man.

(Enter Athena above the temple.)

Ah!
What goddess shows her sunlit face above
the fragrant temple? Mother, let us fly.   1550
We should not see the gods unless the right
is given to us.

ATHENA

No, stay. I am no enemy to flee,
but well disposed, in Delphi as in Athens.
I am Athena, whose name your city bears: 1555
I have come here in haste, sent by Apollo,
who did not think it right to come himself
before you, lest he should be blamed in public
for what has happened in the past; he sent me
to give his message:
                        This woman is your mother,   1560
your father is Apollo; and he gave you
to him to whom he gave you not because
you are his son, but so that he could place you
in a noble house. But when this plan he made
was opened and laid bare, he was afraid
your mother's scheme of murder would succeed,
or she be killed by you, and he found the means   1565
of rescue; but for this, he would have kept
the secret longer and in Athens showed you
Creusa as your mother and himself
the father of her child. But I must end
my task and tell the purpose of my journey.
Now hear Apollo's revelations.   1570

Creusa,

go with your son to Cecrops' land, and then
appoint him to the royal throne; for since
he is descended from Erechtheus, he has
the right to rule my land: and he shall be
renowned through Greece. His sons, four branches from 1575
one stock, shall give their names to land and peoples,
divided in their tribes, who live about my rock.
The first shall be named Geleon, the tribe°
of Hopletes second, then Argades, and one 1580
Aegicores, the name from my own aegis.
At the appointed time, the children born
of them shall colonize the Cyclades,
possess the island cities and the coast,
and thus give strength to my own land of Athens.
They shall live in the two broad plains of Asia
and Europe, which lie on either side the Straits, 1585
becoming famous under this boy's name,
Ionians. Moreover, you and Xuthus
are promised children. First Dorus, whose name
shall cause the town of Doris to be hymned 1590
throughout the land of Pelops. Then Achaeus,
king of the coast near Rhion, who shall mark
a people with his name.

Apollo then

has managed all things well. He made your labor 1595
easy, so that your family would not know;
and when the child was born and you exposed
him in his swaddling clothes, he ordered Hermes
to take him in his arms and bring him here,
and would not let him die, but reared him up. 1600
Now tell no one that Ion is your son,
and Xuthus will be happy in his belief,
while you may go away, Creusa, sure
of your own blessings.—Now farewell you all;

you are delivered of your present evils,
and I confirm: your future holds good fortune.   1605

ION

O Athena, child of mighty Zeus, we have received
what you say on trust. And I believe myself Apollo's
and Creusa's son—and even previously this was credible.

CREUSA

Listen to me. Although before I did not praise him,
now I praise Apollo. For the son he° had neglected   1610
is restored to me; and now this oracle, these doors,
I look upon with joy, though they were hateful once.
Happily I cling to them and bid farewell.

ATHENA

I approve this change, this praise of him.° The gods perhaps
move to action late, but in the end they show their strength.   1615

CREUSA

Son, now let us go.

ATHENA

                          Yes, go, and I will follow you.

ION°

Worthy guardian of our journey . . .

CREUSA

                          . . . and one who loves the city.

ATHENA   (To Ion.)

Mount the ancient throne.

ION

                          That is a worthy prize for me.

                  (Exit Creusa and Ion to the side; exit Athena.)

CHORUS
   O Apollo, son of Zeus and Leto, now farewell.
   He whose house is pressed by trouble should respect the
      gods,   1620
   so preserving courage. For at last good men are honored,
   evil men by their own nature cannot ever prosper.

TEXTUAL NOTES

(Line numbers in some cases are only approximate.)

HERACLES

89: This line is transmitted after line 86 in the manuscript but is placed here by most modern scholars.

119-23: Text uncertain.

191-92: These lines are transposed to after 194 by many scholars, and are rejected by others as an interpolation.

252-74: These lines are assigned by the manuscript to Amphitryon but are given by all modern scholars to the Chorus Leader. Perhaps different sections of this speech are to be assigned to different members of the chorus.

257: Text uncertain.

452: This line is rejected by most scholars as an interpolation.

531-32: The manuscript assigns both of these lines entirely to Megara; some scholars attribute them to Amphitryon.

588-92: These lines are rejected by many scholars as an interpolation.

697: Text uncertain.

762: This line is rejected by most scholars as an interpolation.

845: Text uncertain.

880: It is uncertain whether the reference is to Madness or to Iris; the text may be corrupt.

906-9: The text of these lines and their attribution (to Amphitryon or to the chorus) are uncertain.

955: Text uncertain.

957: Text uncertain.

1009–10: These two lines are transmitted in the manuscript in reverse order.

1022: Text uncertain.

1062: Text uncertain.

1159: This word is missing in the manuscript.

1185–89: Scholars disagree about the proper order of these lines.

1228: Text uncertain.

1241: Probably one line spoken by Heracles, expressing some kind of threat, and one spoken by Theseus in reply are missing here.

1288: Text uncertain.

1291–93: These lines are rejected by most scholars as an interpolation.

1299–1300: These lines are rejected by many scholars as an interpolation.

1311: The manuscript assigns these two lines to Theseus as the beginning of his speech, but most scholars give them to the Chorus Leader instead.

1312: Probably one or more lines spoken by Theseus are missing before this line.

1338–39: These lines are rejected by most scholars as an interpolation.

1366: This line is rejected by most scholars as an interpolation.

1420: Text uncertain.

1421: This line is rejected by most scholars as an interpolation.

THE TROJAN WOMEN

13–14: These two lines are rejected by most scholars as an interpolation.

201: The manuscripts read "the bodies of my sons"; the translation reflects an emendation accepted by most scholars.

261: A word or two seem to be missing here.

383–85: Some or all of these lines are rejected as interpolations by many scholars.

434: After this line, one or more verses seem to be missing; line 435 gives the probable sense.

587–94: Scholars disagree on which of these lines to assign to Hecuba, which to Andromache.

604-5: A word or two seem to be missing from each of these two lines.

634-35: These two lines are rejected by most scholars as interpolations.

638: Text uncertain.

861: After this line, the manuscripts transmit two lines, "For I am Menelaus, I who indeed have toiled much, and the Greek army" (862-63); they are rejected by most scholars as an interpolation.

959-60: These two lines are rejected by some scholars as an interpolation.

961: After this verse many scholars suggest that one or more lines have been lost.

990: The beginning of the name "Aphrodite" sounds like various Greek words for folly or lust.

1090: Text uncertain.

1140: This line is rejected by many scholars as an interpolation.

1211: Text uncertain.

1217: Astyanax's name means etymologically "lord of the city."

1239: Text uncertain.

1240: Text uncertain.

1290: Text uncertain.

1299-1300: Text uncertain.

IPHIGENIA AMONG THE TAURIANS

35-41: Text uncertain.

58: After this line the manuscript transmits two lines (59-60) that are rejected by most modern scholars as an interpolation: "Nor can I apply this dream to my dear ones: for Strophius did not have a son when I was being killed."

83: After this line the manuscript transmits one line (84): "which I suffered wandering throughout Greece." This line is similar to line 1455 and is deleted here by some scholars as an interpolation.

98-100: Text uncertain.

112: After this line the manuscript transmits one and a half lines (113-14) of which the text and translation are uncertain.

115: After this line the manuscript transmits two lines (116–17) which it assigns to Orestes: "We certainly did not come by ship on such a long voyage only to set out again from its limits for home." Scholars are divided whether to maintain that attribution, assign them to Pylades instead, transpose them elsewhere, or delete them.

123–25: Scholars disagree on whether to assign these first three verses to Iphigenia, to the chorus, or to both.

140: After this line the manuscript transmits one metrically defective line (141): "of the famous sons of Atreus." The correct text of these words is uncertain.

150: Text uncertain.

190–97: Text uncertain.

203: Two half-lines may be missing here.

212: After this line the manuscript transmits one line (213): "she bore, she raised, invoked by prayer." The text and meaning of this line are uncertain.

208: This line is transposed here by many scholars.

225: Text and translation uncertain.

258–59: Some scholars transpose these lines so that they come after line 245 or 335, in either case assigning them to the Herdsman.

288–90: Text uncertain.

293: After this line the manuscript transmits one line (294): "which they say the Erinyes emit as imitations." The text and meaning of this line are uncertain and many scholars reject it as an interpolation.

299: Rejected by some scholars as an interpolation.

316: After this line the manuscript transmits one line (317): "and the present disaster near to them." This line is rejected by some scholars as an interpolation.

331: The manuscript reads "stole"; the translation reflects a widely adopted modern emendation.

395: One or two words are probably missing here.

409: Text uncertain.

415: Text uncertain.

427: One word is probably missing here.

451–55: Text and translation uncertain.

515–16: These two lines are transmitted in the manuscript after line 514 and are transposed to after line 510 by many modern scholars.

571: After this line the manuscript transmits three lines (572–74): "There is much turmoil in divine affairs and in those of mortals. He feels grief in one regard only, when, although he is not stupid, he has been convinced by the words of seers and is destroyed as he is destroyed for those who know." The text and meaning of these lines is uncertain.

580: Text uncertain.

587: Text uncertain.

633: Text uncertain.

780–81: The assignment of the speakers for these lines is confused in the manuscript; the translation reflects a plausible modern scholarly correction.

798–99: These lines are assigned by the manuscript to the chorus, but most modern scholars give them to Iphigenia instead.

829: Text uncertain.

867: This line is transmitted after line 866 in the manuscript, where it is attributed to Orestes; it is transposed to after 865 and attributed to Iphigenia by modern scholars.

874: Text uncertain.

895–97: Text and translation uncertain.

907–8: Rejected by some scholars as an interpolation.

914: Text and translation uncertain.

930–36: The manuscript transmits the lines in the order indicated by the numbering; the order in which they are translated here reflects a transposition accepted by most modern scholars.

942–43: Text uncertain.

1050: This line is transmitted in the manuscript between lines 1049 and 1051 and is transposed to after line 1051 by modern scholars.

1052: This line is attributed in the manuscript to Orestes; some modern scholars assign it instead to Iphigenia.

1071: Rejected by some scholars as an interpolation.

1132–36: Text uncertain.

1143–52: Text uncertain.

1214: Iphigenia's words are missing in the manuscript.

1218: Text and translation uncertain.

1249: Text and translation uncertain.

1260: One word is probably missing in the manuscript here.

1309: Text uncertain.

1380: This word is missing in the manuscript and is supplied by modern scholars.

1469: Probably one or more lines are missing here.

1490–91: These lines are assigned to Athena by the manuscript; some scholars give them to the chorus, but it would probably be better to give them to Thoas instead. Lines 1490–96 are suspected by some scholars of being an interpolation.

1497–99: These lines are identical to *The Phoenician Women* lines 1764–66, *Orestes* 1691–93, and *Hippolytus* lines 1466a–c; most scholars reject them here as an interpolation.

ION

1: The text is uncertain, but the meaning is clear.

169: The text of this line is uncertain.

178: A word is missing here in the manuscript, presumably an adjective modifying "shrine."

184–221: The manuscript assigns some parts of this song to Ion, some to the chorus; modern scholars assign it all to the chorus. Probably some parts were sung by different individual members of the chorus.

221: A word is missing here in the manuscript.

237: Before this line a verse may be missing in the manuscript.

285: The exact reading is uncertain.

286: The manuscript reads "He honors, he honors." The translation reflects a widely accepted scholarly emendation.

360: The Greek can just as well mean, "And you miss your unhappy mother?"

374–77: Some scholars reject these lines as an interpolation.

390: The text and meaning of this line are uncertain.

467: Text uncertain.

487: The text of this line and the next one is uncertain.

578–81: Some scholars reject these lines as an interpolation.

593–94: The text is uncertain.

661–63: Ion's name is derived here from a word meaning "going."

697–98: The text of these lines and their exact sense are uncertain.

709–10: A line and a half are missing in the manuscript; the translation reflects the probable meaning.

721: Text and meaning are uncertain.

801: See note on lines 661–63.

802: The manuscript assigns this half line to the Old Man, but many editors give it to the Chorus Leader instead.

828: The text of this line is uncertain. Some scholars reject lines 828–31 as an interpolation.

844–58: Many scholars reject some or all of these lines as being interpolated.

916: Text uncertain.

925: Text uncertain.

991–98: The line numbers indicate the sequence transmitted by the manuscript; modern scholars have rearranged them as indicated to yield a more satisfactory sense.

1071: Text uncertain.

1082–83: Text uncertain.

1098–99: The text of these lines is uncertain.

1107: One line is probably missing in the manuscript at this point.

1117: The following words are rejected by some scholars as an interpolation.

1171: One word is missing in the manuscript here.

1214: One line is probably missing in the manuscript at this point.

1232–34: Text uncertain.

1275–78: Some scholars reject these lines as an interpolation; others transpose them to follow line 1281.

1288: The text and meaning of this line are uncertain.

1300–1303: Many scholars transpose these lines to follow line 1295.

1360: The text of the following sentence is uncertain.

1364–68: Some scholars reject these lines as an interpolation.

1424: The text of these last words and their meaning are uncertain.

1427: The text of this line is uncertain; the translation reflects a widely accepted scholarly emendation.

1489: The text is uncertain here; the translation reflects one plausible scholarly emendation.

1499: Some scholars emend the text of this line to read "You killed me against your will" and assign it to Ion together with the following lines.

1500: The text of these words is uncertain but their meaning is fairly secure.

1579: Some scholars suggest that a line has been lost in the manuscript at this point.

1610: Some scholars emend the text to read "I had neglected."

1614: Text uncertain.

1617 and 1618: These words are assigned in the manuscript to Creusa (if so, then Ion remains silent from line 1608 for the rest of the play); most modern scholars assign them instead to Ion.

GLOSSARY

Abantian: Euboean, referring to the island off the eastern coast of mainland Greece.

Acastus: son of Pelias (the king of Iolcus); brother of Alcestis.

Achaeans: inhabitants of Achaea, a region in Greece on the northern coast of the Peloponnese; sometimes used to refer to all the Greeks.

Achaeus: son of Xuthus and Creusa; legendary founder of the Achaeans.

Acheron: a river or lake of the underworld; more generally, the underworld.

Achilles: son of Peleus and Thetis; father of Neoptolemus; the greatest Greek warrior at Troy.

Aegean: the sea to the east and south of mainland Greece.

Aegicores: one of the four tribes into which the people of Attica were traditionally divided.

aegis: the shield of Athena, displaying the head of a Gorgon in its center.

Aeolian: referring to the Aeolians, one of the four major tribes of ancient Greece.

Aeolus: son of Zeus; father of Xuthus; legendary founder of the Aeolians.

Aetna: a volcanic mountain on the island of Sicily.

Agamemnon: son of Atreus; leader of the Greek army at Troy; brother of Menelaus; husband of Clytemnestra, killed by her and Aegisthus upon his return from Troy; father of Iphigenia, Electra, and Orestes.

Aglaurus: legendary wife of Cecrops; mother of three girls to whom Athena entrusted the baby Erichthonius under condition that they not look upon him; they disobeyed her instructions, went mad, and jumped to their death from the Acropolis.

ailinos: a ritual cry of anguish or mourning.

Ajax: son of Oileus; Greek warrior during the Trojan War, less famous than Ajax, son of Telamon; at Troy's capture he raped the virgin priestess Cassandra, who had sought refuge in the temple of Athena.

Alcaeus: a son of Perseus and Andromeda, and father of Amphitryon.

Alcmene: wife of Amphitryon; mother of Heracles.

Alexander: another name of Paris; son of Priam and Hecuba.

Alpheus: a river in the Peloponnese in southern Greece; it flows along Olympia, the site of an important Greek religious center.

Amazons, Amazonian: a mythical race of warrior women who fought against the Greeks led by Heracles, or, according to another legend, against the Athenians led by Theseus.

Amphanae: a town in the region of Doris in south-central Greece.

Amphion: legendary co-builder of Thebes together with his twin brother Zethus.

Amphitrite: a sea goddess, wife of Poseidon.

Amphitryon: husband of Alcmene, and human father of Heracles.

Amyclae: a town southwest of Sparta in the Peloponnese in southern Greece.

Anaurus: a river in southeastern Thessaly in central Greece.

Andromache: during the Trojan War, the wife of Hector and mother of Astyanax; afterward, the slave concubine of Neoptolemus and mother of a child with him.

Aphrodite: goddess of sexual desire; the beginning of her name sounds like various Greek words for folly or lust.

Apollo: son of Zeus and Leto; twin brother of Artemis; god of archery, prophecy, healing, and poetry; his prophetic seat was at Delphi.

Arcadia: a region in southern Greece in the central Peloponnese.

Ares: god of war.

Argades: one of the four tribes into which the people of Attica were traditionally divided.

Argive: referring to Argos; in general, Greek.

Argos: a city and region in the eastern Peloponnese in southern Greece, not always distinguished clearly from Mycenae.

Artemis: daughter of Zeus and Leto; twin sister of Apollo; goddess of the hunt, childbirth, and virginity, who protected wild animals and boys and girls before they reached adolescence; as "Lightbringer," identified with the moon.

Asia: the western coast of what is now Turkey, also called Asia Minor.

Asopus: a river in Boeotia that flows near Thebes.

Astyanax: young son of Hector and Andromache; hurled from the walls of Troy when the Greeks sacked the city; his name means etymologically "lord of the city."

Athena: daughter of Zeus and Metis; goddess of wisdom and warfare; patron goddess of Athens.

Athens: an important city in the region of Attica in the east-central part of Greece; home of Greek tragedy.

Atlas: a mythical giant said to stand at the far western extremity of the world and to bear the heavens on his shoulders.

Atreus: father of Agamemnon and Menelaus; brother of Thyestes.

Attic: referring to a region of east-central Greece (Attica) dominated by and belonging to Athens.

Aulis: a harbor in eastern Greece in Boeotia, from which the Greek fleet set sail for Troy.

Bacchanalian: referring to the celebrations of the worship of Dionysus.

Bacchus: Dionysus.

Bear: the constellation of Ursa Major.

Bibline: a celebrated wine from Thrace.

Brauron: site of an important cult of Artemis in Attica.

Cadmus: originally a Phoenician prince, mythical founder of the Greek city of Thebes.

Calchas: the most important seer of the Greek army during the Trojan War.

Callichoroe: a spring at Eleusis, a town near Athens, around which girls performed choral dances.

Capherea: a promontory on the southeast coast of Euboea.

Carystus: a town on the island of Euboea off the coast of eastern central Greece.

Cassandra: daughter of Priam and Hecuba; inspired prophetess of Apollo; when Troy was captured, she sought refuge at the temple of Athena but was raped by Ajax, son of Oileus; afterward she was brought home by Agamemnon as his concubine and was murdered by Clytemnestra.

Castalia: a fountain at Delphi at the foot of Mount Parnassus.

Castor: together with Polydeuces (or Pollux), one of the twin sons of Tyndareus; brother of Helen and Clytemnestra; a divinity who protected mariners in distress.

Cecrops: a legendary king of Athens.

Centaurs: mythical savage beings, half-human, half-horse, against whom Heracles waged war.

Cephisus: a major river that waters the plain west of Athens.

Chalcodon: leader of the Abantes, an ancient Ionian tribe who lived on Euboea.

Charon: the mythical boatman who ferried the souls of the dead across the river into the underworld.

Clashing Rocks: the two rocks (Symplegades), located at either side of the Bosphorus at the entrance to the Black Sea; they were said to crash together and crush ships as they tried to pass through.

Clytemnestra: wife of Agamemnon; together with her lover Aegisthus she killed him on his return from Troy; mother of Iphigenia, Electra, and

Orestes, who killed her in revenge for his father's death. Also written Clytaemestra.

Crathis: a river in southern Italy.

Creon: a king of Thebes.

Crete: a large and important Greek island in the southeastern Mediterranean.

Creusa: a legendary queen of Athens, mother of Ion.

Cronion: Zeus as the son of Cronus.

Cyclades: a group of Greek islands in the Aegean Sea.

Cyclopes, Cyclopean: divine craftsmen who were thought to have built the walls of Mycenae, Argos, and other cities.

Cycnus: son of Ares; murderer of travelers until Heracles killed him.

Cynthian: an epithet of Apollo, who was born at Mount Cynthus on Delos.

Cypris, Cyprian: Aphrodite, who was born in the sea near the island of Cyprus.

Danaans: descendants of Danaus; in general, Argives and, more generally, all the Greeks.

Danaus: a hero who was one of the legendary founders of Argos; father of fifty daughters (the Danaids), forty-nine of whom killed on their wedding night the cousins they were obliged to marry.

Dardanian: Trojan.

Dardanus: a hero who was one of the legendary founders of Troy.

Deiphobus: Trojan warrior, son of Priam and Hecuba; after Paris was killed, Deiphobus became the second Trojan husband of Helen.

Delos, Delian: a Greek island, birthplace of Apollo and Artemis and a center of their worship.

Delphi: the major oracle and cult center of Apollo, situated on Mount Parnassus in central Greece.

Demeter: goddess of grains and fertility, mother of Persephone.

Dictynna: a Cretan mountain nymph identified with Artemis.

Diomedes: a giant of Thrace who owned man-eating horses.

Dionysus: son of Zeus and Semele; god of wine, music, and theater; also known as Bacchus.

Dirce: a legendary heroine of Thebes; aunt of Antiope, who was the mother of Amphion and Zethus; also a fountain and river in Thebes.

Dirphys: the tallest mountain on Euboea.

Doris: a region and town in central Greece, traditionally the homeland of the Dorians, one of the four major tribes of ancient Greece.

Dorus: son of Xuthus and Creusa; legendary founder of the Dorians.

Electra: daughter of Agamemnon and Clytemnestra; sister of Iphigenia and Orestes.

Electryon: son of Perseus and Andromeda; king of Tiryns; father of Alcmene.

Enceladus: one of the Giants defeated by the Olympian gods; he was wounded by Athena.

Epeius: Greek warrior, designer of the Trojan horse.

Erechtheus: a legendary king of Athens.

Erichthonius: son of Earth and Hephaestus; a legendary king of Athens.

Erytheia: a city or island off the coast of southwestern Spain.

Euboea, Euboean: referring to a large island off the coast of eastern mainland Greece.

Euripus: the narrow channel of water between the island of Euboea and the Greek mainland at Aulis.

Eurotas: a river near Sparta in the Peloponnese in southern Greece.

Eurystheus: son of Sthenelus; legendary king of Mycenae or Argos; he imposed the twelve labors on Heracles.

fire god: Hephaestus, god of human and natural fire.

Furies: monstrous female divinities of vengeance, who punished especially murder within the family.

Gaia: Earth.

Ganymede: a beautiful Trojan prince, abducted by Zeus to serve as his cup-bearer on Olympus.

Geleon: legendary founder of the Geleontes, one of the four tribes into which the people of Attica were traditionally divided.

Geryon: a monstrous herdsman who lived in the far western part of the Mediterranean; Heracles killed him and stole his cattle.

Giants: children of Earth, also sometimes called Titans, who fought against the Olympian gods and were defeated by them.

Gorgon: a monster produced by Earth to help her children, the Titans; killed by Athena; one of three monstrous snake-women who included Medusa, killed by Perseus; their faces were so terrifying that whoever looked on them was turned to stone.

Graces: companions of Aphrodite, goddesses of all kinds of beauty and charm.

Hades: brother of Zeus and Poseidon; god of the underworld; his name is used synonymously for the underworld itself.

Halae: a site in Attica near Brauron; location of a temple of Artemis Tauropolus.

Hebrus: a large river in northern Greece.

Hecate: goddess associated with witchcraft, night, doorways, crossroads, and the moon; sometimes identified with Artemis.

Hector: the foremost warrior of the Trojans during the Trojan War; a son of Priam and Hecuba; husband of Andromache; he was killed by Achilles.

Hecuba: queen of Troy; wife of Priam, and, according to some accounts, mother of fifty sons and daughters.

Helen: daughter of Zeus (or Tyndareus) and Leda; wife of Menelaus (the brother of Agamemnon); her elopement with Paris caused the Trojan War.

Helicon: a mountain in Boeotia in central Greece associated with the Muses.

Helios: the god of the sun.

Hellas: Greece.

Hellene: Greek.

Hera: wife and sister of Zeus; queen of the gods; goddess of marriage; she had an important cult center at Argos.

Heracles: son of Zeus and Alcmene; the greatest hero of Greek legend, famous for his physical strength, his twelve labors, and his wildness in drinking and sexuality; he was said to have led a first Greek expedition that conquered Troy in the generation before the Trojan War celebrated by Homer.

Hermes: son of Zeus and Maia; the messenger god; god of travelers, contests, stealth, and heralds; he escorted the souls of the dead to the underworld.

Hermione: a town in the eastern Peloponnese in southern Greece, site of a temple of Demeter.

Hesperides: legendary nymphs who tended a beautiful garden at the far western corner of the world near Atlas.

Hill of Ares: the Areopagus, a hill in Athens near the Acropolis, site of an important court of law.

Hippodameia: daughter of Oenomaus. He challenged all suitors of her hand to a chariot race and killed them when they lost; eventually Pelops bribed Oenomaus' charioteer, who sabotaged Oenomaus' chariot so that he was killed during the race, and Pelops married Hippodameia.

Homole: a mountain in Thessaly in central Greece.

Hopletes: one of the four tribes into which the people of Attica were traditionally divided.

Hostile Sea: the Black Sea, traditionally difficult for sailors and inhabited by hostile peoples (the usual Greek name, *Euxeinos*, means "hospitable" and was probably euphemistic).

Hyades: nymphs, daughters of Atlas; sisters of the Pleiades, who like them were turned into a cluster of stars.

Hydra: a mythical monster with many heads that grew back whenever one was cut off; killed by Heracles.

Hymen, or Hymenaeus: god of marriage; wedding song.

Ida: a mountain near Troy, where Paris judged a beauty contest between Hera, Athena, and Aphrodite.

Ilium: Troy.

Iolaus: a nephew and comrade of Heracles who assisted him in many of his exploits.

Ion: son of Creusa and Apollo; legendary king of Athens and founder of the Ionian tribe. Euripides derives his name from a word meaning "going."

Ionian Sea: the sea to the west of Greece and the southeast of Italy.

Ionians: one of the four major tribes of ancient Greece.

Iphigenia: eldest daughter of Agamemnon and Clytemnestra; when adverse winds blocked the Greek fleet at Aulis from sailing to Troy, she was sacrificed to Artemis there by her father (in some versions Artemis spirited her away to the land of the Taurians and put a deer in her place).

Iris: the messenger of the gods.

Ismenus: a river in Boeotia that flows through Thebes.

Isthmus, Isthmian: a narrow strip of land connecting the Peloponnese in southern Greece to the rest of mainland Greece; site of an important religious center and of the large and important city of Corinth.

Ithaca: a western Greek island in the Ionian Sea, home of Odysseus.

Ixion: a mythical criminal who after numerous misdeeds was punished in the underworld by being tied to a fiery wheel that spun forever.

Kore: Persephone (literally, "daughter").

Lacedaemonian: Spartan.

Laconia: a region in southern Greece in the southeastern part of the Peloponnese; Sparta is situated there.

Laertes: father of Odysseus.

Laomedon: Trojan king, father of Ganymede.

Leda: mythical queen of Sparta, wife of Tyndareus; visited by Zeus in the form of a swan, hence the mother of Castor and Polydeuces, and of Helen and Clytemnestra.

Lemnos: an island in the northern part of the Aegean Sea; according to legend, its female inhabitants went mad and killed all their male relatives.

Lerna, Lernaean: a marshy area near Argos; home of the Hydra.

Leto: goddess, the mother of Apollo and Artemis.

Leucothea: a Theban heroine, originally named Ino, who was driven mad by Hera and carrying her son Melicertes jumped into the sea; her son was divinized as Palaemon; both divinities protected sailors.

Libyan: referring to Libya, a region on the southern coast of the Mediterranean.

Ligyan: Ligurian, referring to the western coast of Italy.

Linos: a son of Apollo and a Muse, according to some versions killed by Heracles; personification of funeral dirges.

Long Rocks: cliffs on the northern slope of the Acropolis in Athens.

Loxias: Apollo; the word means "slanting" and may refer to the ambiguity of his oracles.

Lycus: a legendary king of Thebes; another Lycus, a descendant of this first one, later usurped the throne of Thebes.

maenad: a female worshipper of Dionysus.

Maeotis: a sea to the northeast of the Black Sea, now called the Sea of Azov.

Maia: a nymph, who bore Hermes to Zeus.

Maid: another epithet for Persephone.

Maiden of Ilium: Athena.

Megara: wife of Heracles, mother of their three sons.

Menelaus: son of Atreus; brother of Agamemnon; husband of Helen.

Menoeceus: father of Creon.

Mimas: one of the Giants defeated by the Olympian gods; he was burned up by molten metal launched by Hephaestus.

Minotaur: a mythical Cretan monster, half man, half bull, to which every year fourteen young Athenians were sacrificed; killed by Theseus.

Minyan: a legendary primitive people in Greece, defeated by Heracles.

Mount Parnassus: *see* Parnassus

Muses: daughters of Mnemosyne and Zeus, associated with all forms of cultural, especially artistic, musical, and poetic, excellence.

Mycenae: an ancient city in Greece in the northeastern Peloponnese, not always distinguished clearly from nearby Argos.

Myconos: a Greek island in the Aegean sea near Delos.

Mysteries: various esoteric forms of Greek religion involving secrecy, mystic doctrines, and hopes for the afterlife.

Nauplia: a harbor on the eastern coast of the Peloponnese (modern Nafplion).

Nemean: referring to Nemea, a site near Argos; after Heracles defeated a monstrous lion there, he founded the Nemean athletic games.

Neoptolemus: also known as Pyrrhus; son of Achilles; notorious for his brutality at the sack of Troy (he killed Priam at an altar); afterward he took Andromache as slave and concubine, and was later killed at Delphi.

Nereid: a sea nymph, one of the fifty daughters of Nereus.

Nereus: a divinity of the sea, father of the fifty Nereids; famous for his wisdom.

Nisus: legendary king of the city of Megara in Attica.

Odysseus: son of Laertes or Sisyphus; Greek warrior at Troy, famous for his cleverness.

Oechalia: a legendary city of unknown location captured famously by Heracles.

Oenoë: a town on the island of Icaria in the eastern Aegean Sea, home of a famous temple of Artemis.

Oenomaus: *see* Hippodameia

Olympus: a mountain on which the gods make their home, located in Pieria in northern Greece.

Orestes: son of Agamemnon and Clytemnestra; brother of Iphigenia and Electra; he killed his mother to avenge his father, and consequently was pursued by her Furies.

Orion: a legendary monstrous hunter, placed after his death among the stars.

Ouranus: god of the heavens.

Paean: a name for Apollo as a healer and savior; a kind of poem addressed to the god and imploring or celebrating his help.

Palaemon: the son, originally named Melicertes, of Ino (*see* Leucothea).

Pallas: Athena.

Pan: a rustic, musical god dwelling in wild nature and associated with sudden mental disturbances (hence our term "panic").

Parnassus, Parnassian: a mountain above Delphi in central Greece, associated with Apollo and the Muses.

Peirene: a fountain in Corinth.

Pelasgia: Argos.

Peleus: father of Achilles.

Pelias: father of Acastus and Alcestis; half-brother of Aeson, Jason's father, from whom Pelias stole the throne of Iolcus.

Pelion: a mountain in the southeastern part of Thessaly in central Greece.

Pelops: son of Tantalus; a mythical king of the city of Pisa in the Peloponnese in southern Greece. The land of Pelops was the "Peloponnese." *See also* Hippodameia.

Peneus: a river in Thessaly in central Greece.

Pergamum: Troy.

Persephone: daughter of Demeter; wife of Hades and queen of the underworld.

Perseus: legendary hero who killed the Gorgon Medusa; father of Alcaeus; grandfather of Amphitryon; great-grandfather of Heracles.

Phineus: a legendary blind prophet and king of eastern Thrace, on the western shore of the Black Sea; he was persecuted by Harpies, disgusting winged women who stole or befouled his food, until they were driven off by the Argonauts.

Phlegra, Phlegraea: the legendary place in Thrace or southern Italy where Zeus and the other Olympian gods defeated the Giants.

Phocis: a region in central Greece on the northern shore of the Gulf of Corinth.

Phoebus: epithet of Apollo meaning "bright."

Pholoë: a mountain in Arcadia, in the Peloponnese in southern Greece; home of the Centaurs.

Phrygia, Phrygians: a kingdom (and its people) in what is now west central Turkey; often used as a synonym for Troy (and its people).

Phthia: a region in southern Thessaly in north central Greece.

Phthiotis: a region in east-central Greece.

Pisa: a town in the western Peloponnese in southern Greece, near Olympia.

Pitana: a district of Sparta.

Pleiades: nymphs, daughters of Atlas; sisters of the Hyades, who like them were turned into a cluster of stars.

Pluto: Hades.

Polyxena: daughter of Priam and Hecuba; sacrificed by the Greeks to the dead Achilles after the fall of Troy.

Poseidon: brother of Zeus; god of the sea, of horses, and of earthquakes.

Priam: king of Troy; husband of Hecuba; killed by Neoptolemus at the altar of Zeus during the fall of Troy.

Procne: a mythical Athenian heroine who married Tereus, a Thracian king; when she discovered that he had raped her sister Philomela and torn out her tongue to prevent her from disclosing this, she killed their son Itys and served him to Tereus for dinner.

Prometheus: one of the Titans; he helped Zeus give birth to Athena from his head.

Punic: Phoenician, often referring to Carthage and its empire on the north coast of Africa.

Pylades: son of Strophius of Phocis; the loyal comrade of Orestes.

Pythian: belonging to Delphi (where Apollo had killed the monstrous Python).

Rhion: a town in Achaea, a region of western Greece.

Salamis: an island near Athens.

Scamander: a river near Troy.

Scyros: an island of the Sporades group in the Aegean Sea; the home of Neoptolemus.

Scythian: referring to the Scythians, a nomadic barbarian people living to the north and east of the Black Sea.

Simois: a river near Troy.

Sisyphus: legendary founder of Corinth; a trickster figure who famously deceived the gods on multiple occasions and was punished by having to roll a stone up a hill in the underworld that always rolled back down when it neared the summit.

Sown Men: "Spartoi"; according to Theban legend, the original inhabitants of the city sprang from the ground, from the teeth of a dragon that Cadmus sowed.

Sparta, Spartan: referring to an important Greek town in the Peloponnese in southern Greece.

sprouted men: *see* Sown Men

Straits: the Hellespont, the narrow channel of water linking the Mediterranean and the Black Sea and separating Europe from Asia.

Strophius: king of Phocis; father of Pylades; when Clytemnestra and Aegisthus killed Agamemnon, Orestes was rescued and brought to Strophius for safekeeping.

Taenarus: a cape at the southernmost tip of the Peloponnese in southern Greece, where there was said to be an entrance to the underworld.

Talthybius: a herald of the Greek army at Troy.

Tantalid: referring to the descendants of Tantalus.

Tantalus: father of Pelops; founder of the house of Atreus to which Agamemnon and Aegisthus belonged.

Taphians: piratical inhabitants of the island of Taphos in the Ionian Sea off the coast of northwestern Greece.

Taurians: a barbarian people who inhabited the southern coast of the Crimean peninsula on the Black Sea.

Tauropolus: cult epithet of Artemis as she was worshipped at Halae in Attica.

Telamon: Greek hero from the island of Aegina; son of Aeacus; brother of Peleus; father of Ajax and Teucer.

Thebes: a large city in southern Boeotia in central Greece.

Themis: primeval goddess of custom and established law.

Theseus: son of Aegeus and Aethra; the most important hero of Athenian legend; supposedly the first king of a unified Attica.

Thessaly: a large region in the north central part of Greece.

Thoas: king of the Taurians; his name suggests swiftness.

Three-Quart Jug: a festival, called the *Choes* ("Pitchers"), held every year at Athens in honor of Dionysus, at which there was a competition to drink the new wine; each participant had his own table, wine, and three-quart pitcher.

thyrsus: a wand carried by worshippers of Dionysus, made of a fennel stalk with ivy vines and leaves wound around its tip and topped by a pine cone.

Titan: one of the primeval divinities born from Earth and sometimes called Giants, defeated by Zeus, Athena, and the other Olympian gods.

Tithonus: a beautiful Trojan prince, abducted by Eos, goddess of the dawn.

Tritonis: a lake in northern Africa, sacred to Athena.

Trojan: referring to Troy.

Trophonius: Greek seer who was honored at an oracular cave near Delphi.

Troy: city in northwestern Anatolia (now northwestern Turkey), defeated and pillaged by a Greek army.

Twins of Zeus: Amphion and Zethus, the legendary founders of Thebes.

Tyndareus: king of Sparta; husband of Leda; human father of Castor and Polydeuces, and of Helen and Clytemnestra.

Typhon: a mythical monster, born from Earth, who fought against Zeus and the Olympian gods; Heracles is said to have killed a number of Typhon's monstrous offspring.

war god: Ares.

White Shore: an uninhabited island (now called Fidonisi) on the southwest coast of the Black Sea, about thirty miles northeast of the mouth of the Danube in what is now Romania; the ghost of the dead Achilles was thought to haunt it.

wooden horse: a large, artificial horse made of wood containing a number of Greek warriors; when the Trojans brought it into the city the Greek warriors emerged and let the rest of their army into Troy, which they destroyed.

Xuthus: a legendary king of Athens; husband of Creusa; real or putative father of Ion; founder of various Greek tribes through his sons.

Zethus: legendary co-builder of Thebes together with his twin brother Amphion.

Zeus: king of gods and men; father of several of the Olympian gods, including Apollo; also father of Heracles and many other human heroes.